JERUSALEM · BETHANY · AND · BETHLEHEM

COURT OF THE CHURCH OF THE HOLY SEPULCHRE AT EASTER.

·JERUSALEM·
·BETHANY·AND·
·BETHLEHEM·

BY

J. L. PORTER, D.D., LL.D.

President of Queen's College, Belfast;
Author of "Murray's Handbook for Syria and Palestine,"
&c. &c.

THE TOMB OF DAVID — MOUNT ZION

REVIVISCIMUS

SAN RAFAEL CA

Second, facsimile edition
by Reviviscimus
2010

For information, address:
Reviviscimus Press, P.O. Box 151011
San Rafael CA 94915
reviviscimuspress.com

Printed in the
United States of America

Library of Congress Cataloging-in-Publication Data

Porter, J. L. (Josias Leslie), 1823–1889.
Jerusalem, Bethany, and Bethlehem / by J.L. Porter. — Second, complete facsimile ed.

p. cm.

Originally published: Edinburgh; New York: T. Nelson, 1887.
Includes bibliographical references and index.
ISBN 978-1-59731-460-2 (pbk. : alk. paper)
1. Jerusalem—Description and travel. 2. Palestine—Description and travel.
3. Porter, J. L. (Josias Leslie), 1823–1889. I. Title.
DS109.P65 2010
915.694'40434—dc22   2010022663

TO

Her Royal Highness
THE PRINCESS OF WALES,

WITH PROFOUND SENTIMENTS OF RESPECTFUL GRATITUDE,

IS DEDICATED,

BY GRACIOUS PERMISSION,

THIS VOLUME,

CONTAINING PICTURES OF THOSE HOLY PLACES

WHICH HAVE

FOR EIGHTEEN CENTURIES BEEN ENSHRINED IN THE HEARTS

OF ALL CHRISTIANS.

PREFACE.

THE descriptions of JERUSALEM, BETHANY, AND BETHLEHEM given in the following pages are not the results of a single visit to the Holy City. I resided in Palestine for a number of years; and while preparing "Murray's Hand-Book," and revising its several editions, I had occasion repeatedly to examine, with no little minuteness, all places of sacred and historic interest in Palestine, Jerusalem being the chief.

But in addition to my own careful observations on the spot, I have uniformly consulted all available authorities, and I would specially mention one—"The Land and the Book." I look upon it as a storehouse of nearly everything that illustrates the topography of Palestine, and the manners and customs of the people. It is considerably more than a quarter of a century since I first met my esteemed friend, Dr. Thomson, on the side of Lebanon. Even then he was considered one of the highest authorities on the subjects he has since treated of. The illustrated edition of his book is a splendid work, reflecting the highest credit on the venerable author. It is a book that should be in the hands of all students of the Bible. A few of the engravings in this volume are taken from it, but except these the views here given are entirely new in this country. They are chiefly from photographs taken under the superintendence of M. Le Dr. Lortet in a journey to the East.

PREFACE.

In preparing this work I have had before me for constant reference the magnificent publications of the Palestine Exploration Fund.

I have not attempted to write a learned treatise on the topography or history of Jerusalem. My task has been far simpler—to produce a book whose pictures, by pen and pencil, may perchance direct the attention of readers of all classes to scenes of absorbing sacred interest.

J. LESLIE PORTER.

QUEEN'S COLLEGE, BELFAST,
November 1886.

CONTENTS.

FROM JOPPA TO JERUSALEM.

Joppa, ... i	Lydda, ... xvii
Plain of Sharon, ... xv	Kirjath-Jearim, ... xx
Ramleh, ... xv	First View of Jerusalem, ... xxi

JERUSALEM.

The Site of Jerusalem, ... 13	Walls and Gates of the City, ... 61
Jerusalem from the North, ... 17	Walk through the City, ... 67
View from Olivet, ... 18	The Church of the Holy Sepulchre, ... 71
Walk round the Walls, ... 26	The Tombs of Jerusalem, ... 78
The Place of Wailing, ... 39	Tomb of David, ... 83
The Temple and its Courts, ... 43	Absalom's Pillar, ... 88
The "Dome of the Rock," 47	Tombs of the Prophets, ... 90
Site of the Temple, ... 51	Tomb of the Kings, ... 91
Mosque el-Aksa, ... 55	Fountain of the Virgin, ... 93
Cloisters and Porches of the Temple, ... 56	Pool of Siloam, ... 94

OLIVET AND BETHANY.

Sacred Associations of Olivet, ... 97	The Scene of the Ascension, ... 106
Gethsemane, ... 101	Bethany, ... 107

BETHLEHEM.

From Jerusalem to Bethlehem, ... 113	Cave of Adullam, ... 127
Rachel's Sepulchre, ... 115	Etam, ... 131
Bethlehem, ... 116	Pools of Solomon, ... 132

CONTENTS.

FROM JERUSALEM TO BETH-EL.

Sacred and Historic Scenes, ... 138	Beth-horon, ... 144
Mizpeh, ... 139	Beeroth, ... 145
Gibeon, ... 142	Beth-el, ... 146

FROM BETHEL TO AI, MICHMASH, ETC.

Site of Abraham's Camp and Altar, ... 150	Anathoth, ... 161
Ai, ... 152	Gibeah of Saul, ... 162
Michmash and Geba, ... 155	Nob, ... 163

LIST OF ILLUSTRATIONS.

1. Court of the Church of the Holy Sepulchre at Easter, ... *Frontispiece*
2. The Tomb of David—Mount Zion, ... *Vignette*
3. Joppa from the South-West, ... ii
4. Joppa from the North, ... iii
5. School in the Armenian Convent, Joppa, ... vi
6. Dealer in Lanterns, Joppa, ... vii
7. The Plague Gallery in the Armenian Convent, Joppa, ... ix
8. Egyptian Colonists, Joppa, ... x
9. Bead-Sellers, Joppa, ... xi
10. Egyptian Music-Girl, Joppa, ... xiii
11. Fountain of Abu Nabut, ... xiv
12. Ramleh, ... xvi
13. The White Tower at Ramleh, ... xvii
14. Lydda, ... xviii
15. Church of St. George, Lydda, ... xix
16. Church at Kuryet el-Enab (Kirjath-Jearim), ... xxi
17. Street in Jerusalem, ... xxii
18. Panorama of Jerusalem from the Mount of Olives, ... xxiii
19. Olive Trees in the Kidron Valley, ... 10
20. Ancient Wall of Temple Area, East Side, with Muslem Cemetery, ... 11
21. Tower of David, ... 14
22. Jerusalem from the Pool of Hezekiah, ... 15
23. Hebron or Joppa Gate, ... 16
24. The Mosque el-Aksa (South Side), ... 17
25. Jerusalem from the Mount of Olives, ... 19
26. Lower Valley of Jehoshaphat, or Kidron, ... 21
27. View of the Haram Area from beside the Church of St. Anne, ... 23
28. St. Stephen's Gate, ... 26
29. The Golden Gate—Exterior View, ... 27
30. Tombs in the Valley of Jehoshaphat, ... 28
31. Wall at the South-East Angle of the Haram Area, ... 30
32. Pier in the Vaults of the Mosque el-Aksa, ... 32
33. Pillar of Double Gateway under the Mosque el-Aksa, ... 33
34. Jerusalem from Mount Zion—South-West Angle of Haram, ... 34
35. Jewish Family in Mount Zion, ... 35
36. Robinson's Arch, ... 36
37. Jews' Wailing-Place, ... 37
38. At the Place of Wailing, ... 41
39. Pilate's House, overlooking Haram Area, ... 43
40. Remains of Fort Antonia, in Via Dolorosa, ... 44
41. General View of The Mosque of Omar, ... 45
42. Plan of The Dome of The Rock, ... 48
43. A Portico of the Mosque of Omar, ... 49
44. Pulpit on the Platform of the Haram, ... 51
45. Muslem Praying, ... 52
46. Porch of the Mosque el-Aksa, ... 53
47. Dome of Elias in the Haram Area, ... 55
48. Seller of Bracelets in Court of Church of the Holy Sepulchre, ... 57
49. Christian Oil-Sellers, ... 59
50. Zion Gate, ... 62
51. Sheikh of the Lepers, ... 63
52. The Damascus Gate, ... 64
53. House of Dives, ... 65
54. Via Dolorosa, ... 67
55. Porta Judiciaria, ... 68
56. Jews of Jerusalem, ... 69
57. Musician in Café, ... 71
58. Church of the Holy Sepulchre, ... 72
59. Fellahah in Holiday Attire, ... 73
60. Church of the Holy Sepulchre, ... 75
61. Interior of the Church of the Holy Sepulchre, ... 76
62. Chapel of Calvary, or Golgotha, ... 77
63. Tower of Hippicus on Zion, ... 79
64. The Cœnaculum and Tomb of David, ... 83
65. Village of Siloam, ... 87

LIST OF ILLUSTRATIONS.

66. Absalom's Tomb, ... 88
67. Plan of the Tombs of the Prophets, ... 90
68. Church and Tomb of the Virgin, ... 91
69. Plan of the Tomb of the Kings, ... 92
70. Pool of Siloam, ... 95
71. Travellers' Camp, ... 100
72. Gethsemane as it is, ... 102
73. Bethany, ... 105
74. Ain Karim, ... 109
75. Rachel's Tomb—Bethlehem beyond, ... 114
76. Bethlehem, ... 116
77. Church and Convent, Bethlehem, ... 117
78. The Shepherds' Fields, Bethlehem, ... 119
79. Bead-Sellers, Bethlehem, ... 121
80. Worker in Nacre, Bethlehem, ... 122
81. Interior of the Church of the Nativity, ... 123
82. Women of Bethlehem, ... 125
83. Taamirah Arabs, ... 129
84. Solomon's Pools, ... 132
85. Arab Women of the Taamirah Tribe, ... 135
86. Neby Samwîl, ... 140
87. El-Jîb—Gibeon, ... 142
88. Beit-'Ûr el-Fôka—Upper Beth-Horon, ... 144
89. Ruined Church at el-Bîreh—Beeroth, ... 145
90. Beitin—Beth-el, ... 146
91. Wady es Suweinît, near Mukhmâs, ... 155

INTRODUCTION.

FROM JOPPA TO JERUSALEM.

JOPPA is one of the oldest cities in the world. Pliny says it was founded before the Flood; and Josephus attributes its origin to the Phœnicians in the earliest stage of their commercial enterprise. Strabo has another story, making it the scene of Andromeda's exposure to the sea-monster.

But Joppa has a far higher claim upon our attention than could be given by heathen fables, or by even the most extravagant ascription of mythical antiquity and commercial greatness. It was the port of Jerusalem three thousand years ago, when the mariners of Hiram brought down timber from Lebanon for the building of the Temple. It is the port of Jerusalem to this day. Most Western travellers there first touch the sacred soil of Palestine, and thence go forward on their pilgrimage journey to the Holy City.

The first sight of Joppa from the sea is very striking. Its flat-roofed houses rise up, terrace-like, from the dark rocky shore of the Mediterranean, and cover a little rounded hill. Here and there palm-trees, with tall slender stems and graceful feathery tops, spring up among and over the houses; while great orchards of orange, lemon, apricot, and other fruit-trees, surround the town, and spread out far and wide over the adjoining plain.

When one reaches the shore, through barriers of rocks,—rather a difficult and even dangerous task if the wind happens to blow from the west,—he is charmed at once with the quaintness of the streets and houses, the picturesque beauty of the fountains, gates, and Crusaders' walls, and the crowd of people dressed in the costumes of nearly every country of Europe and Asia. The Babel of languages is as strange as the variety of costume. On emerging at last from the gate of the town,—after many a struggle with boatmen, and customs-officers, and dragomans in gorgeous attire,—the matchless luxuriance and verdure of the orchards burst upon the view. They encircle the town, and extend far out into the plain, embowering in their foliage numbers of trim new villas. The views obtained from the terraced roofs of the higher houses of the town, and from some of the old towers along the walls, are singularly rich. The eye roams over a vast sea of verdure, many-tinted and varied in outline, with the palm, the pomegranate, the spreading terebinth, the golden

JOPPA FROM THE SOUTH-WEST.

orange and lemon, and the stately cypress. Beyond the orchards appear wide reaches of the green meadows and corn-fields of the Plain of Sharon; while on the eastern horizon, miles away, is the long range of the Judean hills, delicately coloured with light-gray summits, russet sides, and deep purple glens. It is a grand panorama, and, as it seemed to me, it is a fitting introduction to the traditional and historic glories of the Promised Land.

It is a remarkable fact, and deserving of notice here, that the physical geography of Palestine has largely tended to mould its history and to form the character and habits of its peoples. Each district was originally colonized by a distinct race; and, strange to say, the habits of the races that succeeded during a long course of ages have been more or less conformed to those of their predecessors. The warlike Philistines held, in Bible times, the strong cities of this sea-board plain, battling against streams of invaders from the

JOPPA FROM THE NORTH.

This page is adjacent to a plate and is intentionally left blank.

Assyrians to the Crusaders; and in modern days the sturdy citizens of Gaza and Joppa, and the soldiers behind the ramparts of Acre, have shown much of the same martial spirit in resisting the wily Turk and the veterans of the First Napoleon. The Phœnicians, from their commercial capitals Tyre and Sidon, sent their fleets into all the world; and now the seats of Syrian commerce have only shifted a little north and south along the coast—to Beyrout, Tripoli, and Joppa.

My first view of the plains of Phœnicia, Sharon, and Philistia, was from the sea. From the vessel's deck I looked with as much eagerness as an old Crusader on the white strand, and the sandy downs, and the verdant orchards, and the broad plain, shut in on the east by the pale blue hills of Samaria and Judea. The cape of Carmel, crowned by its convent, bearing to this day the name of Israel's great prophet, was left behind. Cæsarea was passed. Historic names are wonderfully suggestive, especially when connected with sacred history, and when the eye first rests on the places themselves. Memory then becomes a diorama. It brings before us the great events of bygone ages. So it was with me. In succession I seemed to see the ships of Hiram conducting great rafts of cedar and pine along that coast to Joppa. Then came the merchant vessel of Adramyttium leaving the harbour of Cæsarea, while on its deck stood the Apostle of the Gentiles, guarded by Roman soldiers, and with fettered hands waving a last farewell to weeping friends. I saw the proud galleys of the Crusaders bearing down upon the shore, crowded with mail-clad knights, Europe's best and bravest warriors, bent on the recovery of the Holy Sepulchre. And then, when the mental picture of the distant past dissolved, my eye rested on deserted harbours, ruined cities, a desolate shore, silent alike to the bustle of commerce and the din of battle; as if to show that while man is mortal, his glory fleeting, and all his proud works perishable, God's word is true, and his prophetic judgments cannot fail.

Joppa is still a bustling town. It has no harbour, and it is only under favourable circumstances a vessel can ride at the distance of a mile or so from the shore. Under the guidance of a Jew boy I went to the "house of Simon the tanner." It is modern, but may occupy the old site. The Muslem owner holds it sacred, and can still point to tanneries close by. It stands "by the sea-side," as St. Luke tells us;* and from its roof—flat now, as in New Testament times—I looked out on that same great sea upon which the apostle looked when "he went up upon the house-top to pray." The hour, too, was the same—the "sixth hour," or noon. There was something to me deeply impressive in being thus brought, as it were, into immediate connection with that wondrous vision which the Lord employed as a key to open the Gentile world to Christ's gospel.

The streets of Joppa, like those of all Oriental towns, are narrow and crooked. Winding along them, one sees artisans at work making lamps and lanterns and little tin

---

*Acts x. 6.

vessels, pots and pans, as rude in workmanship and primitive in form as those used by Simon the tanner. The workmen squat like tailors while pursuing their handicraft, and not unfrequently their children sit and play on the ground beside them, as is shown in the accompanying picture. All is done in the open air, the shop front, or shutter, being turned up to shade from the sun's rays.

I had heard of the Armenian convent and schools, and paid them a visit. The convent is a solid building of modern date, with arched cloisters round an open court. Here was the teacher with his conical Persian cap and long dark robe, like a figure taken from one of the monuments

School in the Armenian Convent, Joppa.

of Nineveh. He dictated a lesson to a class of dark-eyed, intelligent-looking children. In another part of the building is a heavy arched gallery, bearing the ominous name of the Plague Gallery, possibly derived from its use by Napoleon I. as a plague hospital during his occupation of the city.

On my way back to the gate I passed an open shop, where dealers in beads from Bethlehem, and relics from the Holy Sepulchre, and ornaments of olive-wood and mother-of-pearl, were busily engaged vending their wares. They never think of rising when a customer appears. They sit high on a shelf of their raised stall, and quietly reach for

DEALER IN LANTERNS, JOPPA.

This page is adjacent to a plate and is intentionally left blank.

anything that may be asked for. A native woman is here seen, as I have seen many a one in Joppa and Jerusalem, sitting on a rude bench, clad in her long and wide white *azâr*, which resembles a large calico sheet; on her face is the dark veil, concealing her features, but leaving exposed the long rows of coins which hang down on each side of her face, like the chain of a dragoon's helmet. The azâr is so made that it can be easily thrown back to give perfect freedom to the arms, and as easily put on again when concealment is desired. It is doubtless a similar style of robe to that of which we read in the Book of Genesis,* when Abraham's servant returned from Mesopotamia with a wife for Isaac: "And Rebekah lifted up her eyes, and when she saw Isaac, she lighted off the camel....And she took a veil, and covered herself." An Arab maid would do the same at the present day.

THE PLAGUE GALLERY IN THE ARMENIAN CONVENT, JOPPA.

Joppa recalls some stirring events, both sacred and civil. The modern name *Yafa* is just the Arabic form of the Hebrew *Japho*, mentioned by Joshua† as a border town of the tribe of Dan, and several times referred to as the port of Palestine. The word signifies "beauty," and was probably descriptive, like so many other Hebrew names, for the site is beautiful. From Joppa Jonah sailed in a ship of Tarshish, when attempting to "flee from the presence of the Lord."‡ To it St. Peter came across the Plain of Sharon from Lydda, and raised Tabitha from the dead. Under the Maccabees it played an important part in the history of Palestine. It was then strongly fortified, and was considered one of the chief defences of the western sea-board of Israel. It was subsequently captured and destroyed by the Emperor Vespasian, because it had become a

*Gen. xxiv. 64.   †Joshua xix. 46.   ‡Jonah i. 3.

den of pirates. The Crusaders under Godfrey took it; but it was retaken by Saladin, and its fortifications destroyed. Richard Cœur-de-Lion soon afterwards drove out the Saracens, and laid the foundations of the present ramparts. It has thus a special interest for the English traveller, who will not fail to look with some feeling of pride upon the remains of the defensive works of our lion-hearted but unfortunate king. During the eighteenth century Joppa was sacked no less than three times—the last time, in 1799, by Napoleon. The massacre of its garrison after capitulation will for ever leave a dark stain upon the memory of that great but unscrupulous monarch.

The *road from Joppa to Jerusalem* is the best in Palestine; in fact it may be said to be the only road in the country, for all others are merely bridle-paths, sometimes more like goat-tracks.

EGYPTIAN COLONISTS, JOPPA.

The present road, thanks to French influence and money, is fit for wheeled conveyances, though the drive will call forth many a groan from those of delicate frames or weak nerves. But the scenery is fine; and the villages, people, ruins, and historic associations are sufficient to draw away the attention from physical discomfort. At first we wind through gardens of vegetables and groves of fruit-trees. Many imposing houses have recently been built; and we have all around us evidences of active life and reviving prosperity. Colonists from America, Germany, and even from Egypt, have settled here, attracted by a soil of unsurpassed fertility and a grand climate. Nowhere in the world are the orange-groves more luxuriant or the fruit of finer flavour. As we pass along we may notice the Egyptians at work in the fields, with their yokes of oxen and their ploughs so rude and primitive in design that it might be supposed they had come down

BEAD-SELLERS, JOPPA.

This page is adjacent to a plate and is intentionally left blank.

unchanged from the days of Abraham. The ploughman, too, carries his goad—a weapon apparently better fitted for a lancer than a peaceful husbandman. After examining the size and make of one of those goads, I did not think the story of the sacred historian so very wonderful, that Shamgar, the Israelitish judge of old, should have slain six hundred men with an ox-goad.

EGYPTIAN MUSIC-GIRL, JOPPA.

The Egyptians irrigate their gardens and fields as they were accustomed to do on the banks of the Nile; drawing the water, however, not from their grand river, but from wells, of which they have sunk numbers in the plain. In their train troops of music-girls have come, to enliven the hard monotony of daily toil, and to celebrate the successful ingathering of harvest and vintage. At marriages, and at family festivals of every kind, and in all times of public rejoicing, the music-girls of Egypt and Syria lead the song and the dance, while maids and matrons of town and village often join in the refrain. I have seen those dances, and I have heard the choruses of human voices accompanied by the tambourine and little drum. The excitement was intense. And when sitting on such occasions by the shore of the Mediterranean, in Philistia or Sharon, or by the Sea of Galilee, or the banks of the Jordan, I could almost have fancied I was witnessing that scene at the Red Sea when, after the destruction of the Egyptian host, "Miriam took a timbrel in her hand; and all the women went out after her with timbrels and with dances:" and as they sang, Miriam took up the refrain: "Sing ye to the Lord, for he hath triumphed gloriously; the horse and his rider hath he thrown into the sea."*

The music-girls dress with much taste and even splendour. They are literally covered with gold and silver and jewels—head, ears, neck, breast, arms, fingers, ankles, and even toes,

FOUNTAIN OF ABU NABUT.

sparkle and tinkle as they move in the dance. One would almost imagine that the prophet Isaiah had taken his long catalogue of the articles of female attire from some gay daughter of Zion, "with stretched forth neck and wanton eyes, making a tinkling with her feet," similar in carriage and dress to the Egyptian belle figured on preceding page. It is possible, indeed easy, with such a picture before the eye, to understand the meaning and significance of "the bravery of their anklets, and the net-works, and the crescents; the pendants, and the bracelets; the head tires, and the ankle chains, and the sashes, and the amulets; the rings, and the nose jewels; the festal robes, and the mantles; and the turbans, and the veils." All this gorgeous display of olden days has been perpetuated. We see it now as the prophet saw it nearly three thousand years ago in the same country, and probably under like circumstances.

*Ex. xv. 20.

Not far from the main road is an interesting fountain among gardens—evidently an ancient site, for there are Jewish tombs, in which lamps and vases of terra-cotta have been discovered. The old name has been forgotten, and it is now dedicated to a certain Muslem santon called Abu Nabut.

Emerging at length from the orange-groves, the Plain of Sharon is before us, stretching away in green meadows and corn-fields, dotted here and there with a clump of trees and a half-ruined village, to the foot of the Judean hills. One must admit that there is a charm in this great plain entirely independent of hallowed associations. True, we cannot forget that over it, almost in our path, St. Peter travelled on his way from Lydda to Joppa; and further north, within range of vision, St. Paul was escorted by Roman soldiers from Antipatris to Cæsarea.* But looking upon that plain as it is, we cannot but feel that it is a landscape which, like a picture by Claude—soft, rich, glowing in varied colours—never passes from the memory. In the far distance we can just distinguish the pale blue top of Carmel. Before us, on the east, is the long range of Samaria and Judah; the rounded summits tinged, as evening approaches, with the golden rays of the sun; and the deep purple shadows of the ravines throwing out in bold relief the ruined towns and castle-like villages that crown each cliff and projecting ridge. On the right, a gentle swell in the plain conceals Philistia; but that swell is clothed with the orchards of Ramleh, whose minarets and tall white tower shoot up from the dense foliage. If we turn and look westward, we see, beyond the gardens and groves of Joppa, the Mediterranean gleaming like a mirror under the bright sky.

Sharon and Philistia constitute the garden of Palestine. Along the entire sea-board are white sandy downs. Within these is the broad plain reaching from Carmel to the "Wilderness of Wandering." Its flat surface is occasionally broken by low mounds, on which lie prostrate and desolate the ruins of famous old cities. Spurs from the hills of Judah run out far into the plain, carrying with them their rocks and jungles of dwarf trees and shrubs, and leaving between picturesque winding vales. Such is Sharon, and such is Philistia. The latter is in many respects a grand country; and it was defended by its old inhabitants with a devotion and a heroism rarely equalled. The Philistine warriors could dash across the unbroken plain in their chariots of iron; but when they attempted to penetrate the mountain defiles they were overmatched by the hardy, active Jewish infantry. It is a singular fact that the name Palestine, long so honoured, is derived from the hereditary enemies of Israel, the *Philistines*.

RAMLEH is now before us, a bustling little town of some three thousand people. Its houses are substantial, and its streets wider and cleaner than in most Oriental towns. There are two buildings of considerable interest;—a church of the Crusading age, now a

---

*Acts xxiii. 31.

mosque; and a tall tower, visible over the whole Plain of Sharon. Of the former Lieutenant Conder writes: "It consists of nave and two aisles, with the principal and side apses, and with seven bays of clustered columns. The nave has a clerestory, forty feet high. The spaces between the piers are irregular. This is not uncommon in Crusading work." The church stands on the eastern side of the town.

About a quarter of a mile west of the town is the *White Tower*, surrounded by the ruins of a large mosque. The tower, now isolated, is square, and beautifully built. The angles are supported by slender buttresses, and the sides taper upwards in stories. A winding staircase

RAMLEH.

leads to the top, where it opens on an external stone gallery. The height is about one hundred and twenty feet. An Arabic inscription over the door of the tower ascribes its erection to Sultan Mansûr, and gives a date equivalent to A.D. 1318. The view from the top is very fine, commanding the whole of Ramleh and the gardens out to Lydda, as well as the great road westward to the orchards of Joppa, and eastward to the defile which leads to Jerusalem.

A recent tradition would identify Ramleh with the *Ramah* of Samuel. But though the names bear some resemblance to each other in form and sound, there is no real similarity. *Ramleh* means "sandy;" Ramah, "a height" or "hill." I can find no historic reference to Ramleh previous to the ninth century, when an Arab historian tells us it was founded by the Khalif Suleiman, after he had destroyed Lydda. It was occupied by the Crusaders; and at a great feast held here in A.D. 1099 it is said that they adopted St. George as their patron saint.

THE WHITE TOWER AT RAMLEH.

LYDDA, the *Lod* of the Old Testament, the *Diospolis* of the later Greeks, and the *Ludd* of the modern Arabs, lies about three miles north of Ramleh. I paid my first visit to it many years ago, but that visit still remains a bright spot on my memory. I was staying with some friends in the convent of Ramleh, and we walked over to the neighbouring town. The sun was already low in the west when we entered the broad avenue-like road that leads from Ramleh to Lydda. It was a beautiful evening—the sky cloudless, the atmosphere transparent as crystal. The sunbeams fell slanting on the thick foliage of the orange and apricot trees, here gilding the topmost leaves, and yonder shooting in lines of gold through the openings. The sea breeze was just setting in. Now it played among the rustling branches of the tall palms, and anon it came down for a moment and breathed its balmy breath in our faces. The road, covered deeply with red sand, is lined with orchards, in which were orange, lemon, peach, pomegranate, and carub trees, intermixed with the palm, walnut, and sycamore; and enclosed within huge hedges of cactus, whose luscious fruit, clinging quaintly to the sides of the great thick leaves, was now almost ripe. A pleasant walk of three-quarters of an hour brought us to Ludd. I have often been sadly disappointed on approaching an old Bible city, which fancy had somehow decked in the choicest beauties of nature and art, but which reality transformed into mud huts on a rocky hill-side. It was not so with Lydda. Even now, though its glory has faded, it has an imposing look. It is embowered in verdure; olive groves encircle it and stretch far out on the adjoining plain. Near the houses vines creep over the garden walls, and graceful palms spring up among the houses.

The village stands on a gentle eminence; and high above its terraced roofs rise the splendid remains of the church of England's patron saint. Lydda, tradition says, was the native town of St. George; and England's chivalrous king, the lion-hearted Richard, built in his honour this noble church, the ruins of which form the chief attraction of the place. The walls and part of the groined roof of the chancel *remained* standing when I was first there, and also one lofty pointed arch, with its clustered columns and white marble capitals, rich in

LYDDA.

carving and fretwork. Now, alas! they are gone. Vandal Greeks destroyed the beautiful Crusading work in converting it into that hideous building which at present occupies the site. On the foundations of the western end of the ancient church a mosque has been erected with a tall but ugly minaret. We climbed to the top of the crumbling wall of the church, and there sat down to read the story of St. Peter's visit.* The whole village was before us. The apostle had been away on one of his missionary tours in the hill country of Samaria—among those hills which we saw in the distance; and "he came down to the saints which dwelt at Lydda." He *came down* through the defiles of those hills, and he travelled across that rich Plain of Sharon, and up the gentle ascent to this old town. The saints seem to have heard of his coming, and they

*Acts ix. 32-39.

met him as he entered, and told him of the suffering of poor paralytic Æneas; and the miracle of healing then performed at his bedside was such as the people had never before witnessed. Æneas had been confined to his bed eight years; "for he was palsied. And Peter said unto him, Æneas, Jesus Christ healeth thee: arise, and make thy bed. And straightway he arose." As the words of the apostle reached his ears, divine power operated on his body. The wondrous tidings spread from mouth to mouth, from group to group, from town to country. All eagerly inquired;

Church of St. George, Lydda.

many probably doubted; but when they saw the healed paralytic, faith triumphed: "And all that dwelt at Lydda and in Sharon saw him, and they turned to the Lord." The joyful news soon found its way to Joppa, ten miles distant; and then the mourning friends of the charitable Dorcas despatched quick messengers to tell Peter of her death, half hoping that even she might not be beyond the reach of his wondrous power. Peter delayed not, but set out at once across that western plain on another journey of mercy.

Lydda was afterwards called *Diospolis*, by which name it is frequently mentioned in ecclesiastical history. It became the seat of a Latin bishop—a distinction it still retains. Here St. George was first honoured. The earliest calendars relate that he was born in

Lydda; that he suffered martyrdom in Nicomedia; and that his body was brought to his native town, where a church was erected and dedicated to him.

The road from Ramleh to Jerusalem runs eastward over the plain, passing the sites of several Bible cities. The first is the long-lost royal city of Gezer, whose king was slain by Joshua when making an attempt to relieve Lachish.* It stood, like most of the old cities of Canaan, on the top of a hill. Now, a Jerusalem merchant has built a house upon it. Next we have the village of *Latrôn,* which a late tradition makes the birthplace of the "penitent thief;" probably from the supposed identity of the Latin word *latro,* "thief," and Latrôn. Next we pass, on the side of a hill, *Amwas,* identified by some with *Emmaus,* where our Lord, after the resurrection, met and conversed with the two disciples. The position, however, does not agree with the Gospel narrative. Emmaus was only "threescore furlongs" from Jerusalem; this village is one hundred and sixty. Next comes *Yalo,* unquestionably the site of the *Ajalon* of Joshua,† which gave its name to the neighbouring long valley, the scene of the memorable pursuit and slaughter of the kings. The wonderful words of the great leader will here recur to us as we look up the vale to the mountain heights over it:—

> "Sun, stand thou still upon Gibeon;
> And thou, Moon, in the valley of Ajalon.
> And the Sun stood still, and the Moon stayed,
> Until the nation had avenged themselves of their enemies."

The hill country of Judah is now before us, rising in rocky banks and long terraced slopes, thinly clothed with shrubs of ilex, hawthorn, and wild rose. The road winds up the ravine of Wady Aly, crosses a broad rugged ridge, and then descends abruptly into a picturesque upland vale, where, amid groves of olives and terraced vineyards, stands the large and prosperous village of Kuryet el-Enab.

Kuryet el-Enab is the *Kirjath-jearim* of the Bible, the modern "village of grapes" having taken the place of the ancient "village of forests;" for such is the meaning respectively of the Arabic and of the Hebrew name. Beside the village is a Gothic church, used for many years as a stable by the noted bandit chief Abu-Ghaush, but now cleared out. Some traces of frescoes of saints and angels may still be seen on the walls. It was probably built during the Crusades. A Franciscan convent was attached to it.

Kirjath-jearim calls up some interesting and stirring incidents of Jewish history. It was one of the cities of the Gibeonites, who, by a clever trick, beguiled Joshua into a league.‡ It was an original high-place of Baal, hence its name Kirjath-baal.§ When the ark of the covenant was restored to Israel, after its capture by the Philistines, it was

---

*Joshua x. 33.   †Joshua xix. 42.   ‡Joshua ix. 17.   §Joshua xv. 60.

brought up to this town, and placed in "the house of Abinadab in the hill."* It remained there until it was removed by king David to the Holy City. As we pass along the road to Jerusalem we are in the track of that wonderful procession, when the ark was set upon a new cart, "and David and all the house of Israel played before the Lord with all manner of instruments made of fir wood, and with harps, and with psalteries, and with timbrels, and with castanets, and with cymbals."†

CHURCH AT KURYET EL-ENAB (KIRJATH-JEARIM).

Kirjath-jearim is just about sixty furlongs from Jerusalem, and it has been suggested that it may perhaps be identical with that village (Emmaus) which occupies such an important place in Gospel history. Changes of name were not uncommon in olden times, nor are they uncommon at present, in Palestine. The earliest name of this village appears to have been Baalah; then it became Kirjath-baal; then it was shortened into Kirjath; then again lengthened into Kirjath-jearim; then, in modern days, it became Kuryet el-Enab; and it is now more generally known as Kuryet Abu-Ghaush. In New Testament times it may have been called Emmaus; this, however, is only a conjecture. Of the real site of Emmaus we have no positive knowledge.

We cross the great valley of Beit Hanina, and at length reach the top of the broad, bleak ridge where we gain our first view of the Holy City. It was disappointing to me when I saw it thirty years ago; it is even more disappointing to those who see it now. Then the embattled city wall stretched in full view across the white crowns of limestone, with the great towers of the Jewish Citadel in its centre, the domes and minarets of the city rising over it, and the rounded ridge of Olivet away beyond. These had at least an

*1 Sam. vii. 1.   †2 Sam. vi. 3-5.

Oriental look. Now they are in a great measure concealed by modern buildings of questionable taste;—on the left, the Russian church, and the convents and hospices, which look like factories; on the right, the square, featureless school of the Prussian deaconesses; in front, white villas, and almshouses, and poor rustic cafes. In some respects Jerusalem is improving. Life and property seem to be almost as safe outside as inside the walls. But the romance is gone. The City of the Great King, the Holy City of the Crusaders, the picturesque City of the Saracens and Turks, is at the present time almost covered and concealed by the tasteless structures of modern traders and ambitious foreign devotees. Holy names remain, however. Holy places cannot be obliterated—Zion and Moriah, Olivet and the Kidron, bid defiance to time and man.

STREET IN JERUSALEM.

This page is adjacent to a plate and is intentionally left blank.

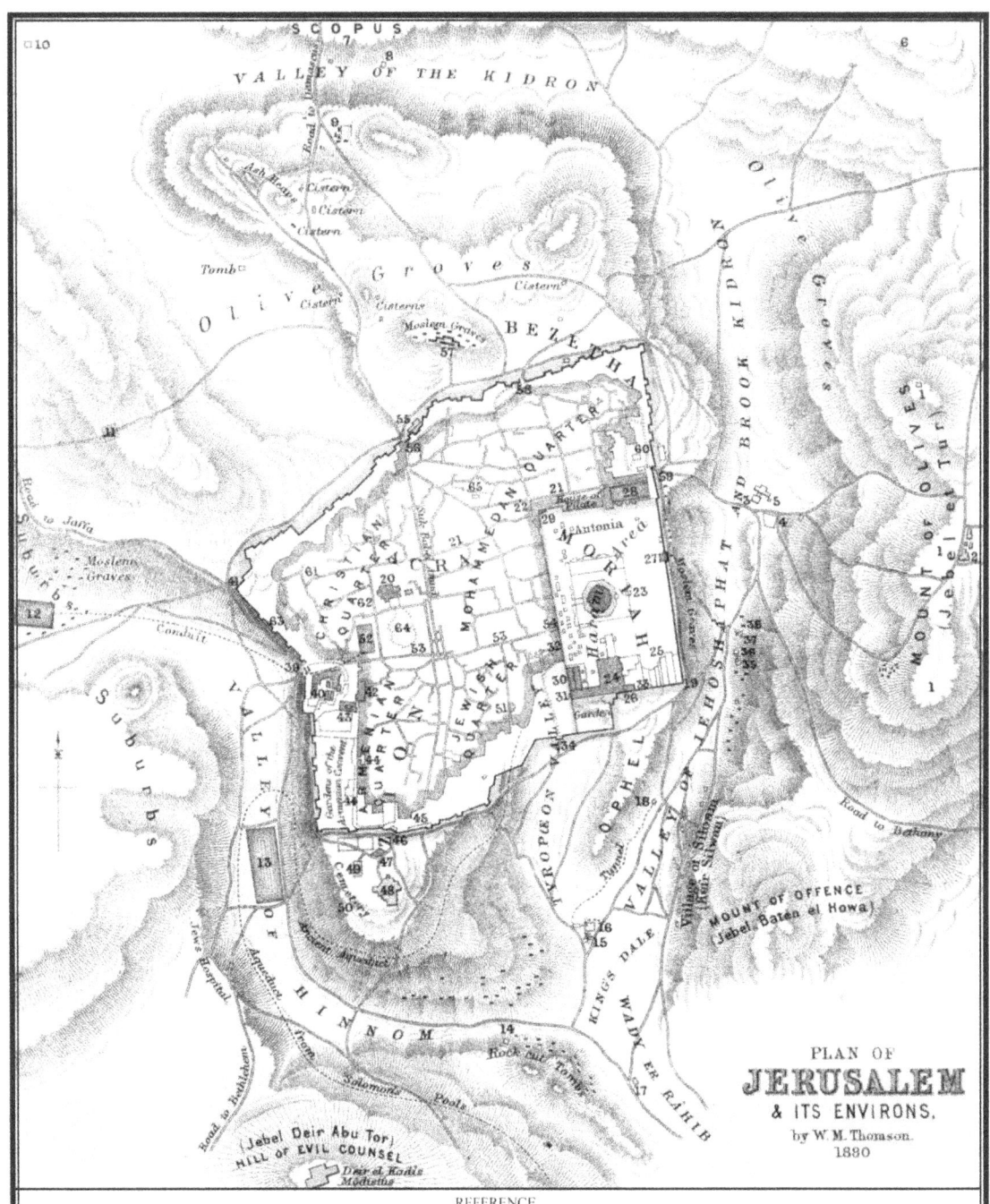

PLAN OF JERUSALEM & ITS ENVIRONS,
by W. M. Thomson. 1880

REFERENCE

1. Mount of Olives
2. Church of the Ascension
3. Church of the Virgin
4. Garden of Gethsemane
5. Grotto of the Agony
6. Nob
7. Scopus
8. Tombs of Simeon and Just & of the Sanhedrin
9. Tombs of the Kings
10. Tombs of the Judges
11. Russian Buildings
12. Upper Pool of Gihon
13. Lower Pool of Gihon
14. Potter's Field
15. Isaiah's Tree
16. Pool of Siloam
17. En-rogel
18. Fountain of the Virgin
19. South-eastern Angle of the Haram
20. Holy Sepulchre
21. Via Dolorosa
22. Ecce Homo Arch
23. Dome of the Rock & Haram Area
24. Mosk of el Aksa
25. Vaults
26. Solomon's Porch
27. Golden Gate
28. Pool of Bethesda
29. Tower of Antonia
30. Wailing-place of the Jews
31. Robinson's Arch
32. Wilson's Arch
33. Double, Triple, Single Gates, closed
34. Gate of the Moors
35. Tomb of Zechariah
36. Tomb of St. James
37. Tomb of Absalom
38. Tomb of Jehoshaphat
39. Jaffa Gate
40. Tower of David, Hippicus
41. Castle of Goliath
42. English Church
43. Barracks
44. Armenian Convent
45. Lepers Village
46. Zion Gate
47. House of Caiaphas
48. The Cœnaculum, & Tomb of David
49. Greek, Latin, Armenian & American Burial-grounds
50. English School, & English & German Burial-grounds
51. Jewish Synagogue
52. Pool of Hezekiah
53. David Street
54. Saracenic Fountain
55. Cotton Grotto
56. Damascus Gate
57. Grotto of Jeremiah
58. Gate of Herod, closed
59. St. Stephen's Gate
60. Birket Hammâm Sitty Meryam
61. Latin Convent
62. Greek Convent
63. Latin Patriarchate
64. Hospital of St. John & el Mûristân
65. Austrian Hospice

JERUSALEM ILLUSTRATED.

THERE is no city in the world like Jerusalem. In and around it cluster the stirring memories of full four thousand years. Every spot is "haunted holy ground," on which may be learned a lesson of sacred history. The hills of Zion, Moriah, and Olivet; the valleys of Kidron and Hinnom; the colossal walls of the old Temple area; the massive towers of David's citadel; the pools of Siloam and Hezekiah; the venerable olives of Gethsemane; the rock-hewn tombs of Tophet and Aceldama—recall events unparalleled. Patriarchs, prophets, and apostles, and ONE infinitely greater and holier than them all, seem to rise before us as we visit the shrines, and tread the streets, and wander "among the mountains round about Jerusalem." The impress of their acts and teachings, of their noble lives and sufferings, lingers still on each well-defined spot, and carries the mind away back to the very presence of the Great and the Good.

My own visits to Jerusalem were to me like a new revelation. The sight of its "holy places" was more instructive and far more deeply impressive than long years of study. Sacred history, so familiar even in boyhood, but which ever appeared to a large extent ideal and almost floating in a kind of cloudland, assumed the clearness and startling vividness of real life. The actors rose up before the mind's eye on the old stage:—"Melchizedek, king of Salem," taking "forth bread and wine" to Abram, and blessing him.* David, in his flight from Absalom, crossing the Kidron, going "up barefoot by the ascent of Mount Olivet"—the beaten path which I followed and thousands still follow—weeping "as he went up;" then turning at a well-marked point, on the top of the mount, where he worshipped God."† Our Lord also driving the buyers and sellers from the Temple court, now the court of the Great Mosque; and then after the lesson on the widow's "two mites,"‡ he goes over the Kidron and up the side of Olivet, along the main road to Bethany, to a point where the whole city was spread out before him, as

*Gen. xiv. 17-19. †2 Sam. xv. 30-32. ‡Mark xii. 41-44.

one can see it this day; and there his disciples, with natural Jewish pride, say, "Master, see what manner of stones and what buildings are here!" And he replied, "Seest thou these great buildings? there shall not be left one stone upon another, that shall not be thrown down."* We see, as we stand on the spot, that the prophetic words have been fulfilled to the letter. The Temple is gone, and the massive encircling wall of its court, broken and defaced, alone remains to mark the site.

We follow Jesus, on a later occasion, down to the bottom of the Kidron, in among a grove of old olives, to the "place called Gethsemane;" and there we seem to witness his agony, and to

OLIVE TREES IN THE KIDRON VALLEY.
(*Near the Garden of Gethsemane*)

hear whispered through the gloom: "O my Father, if it be possible, let this cup pass from me: nevertheless not as I will, but as thou wilt."†

It was thus I saw life-pictures of sacred scenes, and learned life-lessons of sacred history. It is not given to every one to visit the Holy City, but "PICTURES OF JERUSALEM," if faithfully drawn with pen and pencil, go far, I think, to supply the place of personal inspection. Photographs have done much to make holy sites familiar in every

*Mark xiii. 1, 2.   †Matt. xxvi. 39.

ANCIENT WALL OF TEMPLE AREA, EAST SIDE, WITH MUSLEM CEMETERY.

Golden Gate.

Tower of Antonia.

This page is adjacent to a plate and is intentionally left blank.

Christian household; and I venture to hope that those which are so artistically transferred to these pages may serve to bring Bible scenes and Bible stories still more vividly before the reader.

THE SITE OF JERUSALEM.

THE Holy City stands on the broad summit of a mountain ridge, surrounded by bare crowns of white limestone, with bare valleys between. White rocks project from the scanty soil, and the soil itself is almost as white as the rocks, save where, here and there, a little fountain trickles, or a vine shoots out its long tendrils, or a dusky olive raises its rounded top. There is no beauty or grandeur in the scene. The mountain ridge descends westward in rocky declivities, scantily clothed with dwarf trees and copse, and occasionally terraced vineyards, to the plain of Sharon, two thousand seven hundred feet below. On the east it breaks down more abruptly in a barren, rugged wilderness of gray scaurs and white cliffs, nearly four thousand feet, to the profound valley of the Jordan, where the Dead Sea lies like a disc of molten silver.

Two ravines seam the broad summit of the ridge. At first, on the north, they are but gentle depressions; but gradually they grow deeper and deeper—that on the east descending in nearly a straight line, the other curving sharply round and at last joining it. The former is the Kidron, or Valley of Jehoshaphat; the latter, Hinnom; and the point of junction is the Tophet of the Bible,—a spot of horrible associations. Between the Kidron and Hinnom, on a double ridge, stands Jerusalem.

The eastern ridge culminates towards the south in Mount Moriah, crowned of yore with the Temple of Jehovah—crowned now with the beautiful building which for twelve centuries has usurped the sacred spot, the Mosque of Omar, one of the holiest shrines of the False Prophet. The western ridge was the site of the Salem of Melchizedek; of the stronghold of the Jebusites; of the citadel and palace of David; and its most conspicuous and interesting building is now David's Tower, a massive keep of Cyclopean masonry, which may date back to the time of the Jewish monarchy.

Between the two ridges is a smaller valley, now filled to the depth of a hundred feet or more by the ruins of the old city—indeed, of a succession of old cities. In ancient times it was spanned by a huge bridge, the foundations of which were recently brought to light, fifty feet beneath the present surface, by the excavations of the Palestine Exploration Society. The abutments of one of its arches were discovered by Dr. Robinson fifty years ago, and have since attracted the attention of all travellers. To this bridge, and to the Tyropœon Valley which it spanned, and to the remarkable places in it, I shall refer more particularly hereafter.

All around the site of Jerusalem are higher ridges—nothing, however, that could be called mountains, only rounded crowns—overtopping, at the distance of three-quarters of a mile or so, the summits of Zion and Moriah. There are occasional depressions, through which we get a glimpse of the country beyond. One opening on the east, by the shoulder of Olivet, exposes, in the far distance, the delicate purple tints of the mountain-chain of Moab, as if to connect the country of Ruth with the city of David. This general contour of the environs is partially seen in

TOWER OF DAVID.
(*On Mount Zion.*)

the accompanying picture, taken from the brow of Zion, near the Pool of Hezekiah. In the centre is the Church of the Sepulchre, with its flat dome; and near it, on the right, is a minaret, with which is connected an interesting tale of Muslem magnanimity, all the more remarkable because of its rarity. When Jerusalem capitulated to Omar, one of the terms was that the Christians should retain their churches. After the Khalif entered the city he was conversing with the Patriarch when the Muslem hour of prayer came. Omar asked for a place to pray. He was told to pray in the Church of the Sepulchre; but refused, and chose a spot at some distance. He afterwards said to the Patriarch: "Had I prayed in the church, the Muslems would have seized it, and in spite of all you might allege to the contrary, they would have said, 'This is where Omar prayed, and we will pray here also.'" Then, calling for pen and paper, he wrote a command that Muslems should only pray on the spot one at a time. The minaret stands upon that spot.

I have said that there is no grandeur or beauty in the environs of Jerusalem. The city is built on the broad summit of a mountain-chain, and is encircled by bleak ridges a little higher

JERUSALEM FROM THE POOL OF HEZEKIAH
(*Ridge of Olivet in Background.*)

than the site, so that the words of the Psalmist are true, whether we interpret them as referring to the general mountain-chain on which it stands, or to the circuit of ridges encompassing the site:—

"Jerusalem, mountains encompass her,
Jehovah encompasseth his people."*

The traveller, on approaching from the west, is grievously disappointed at the first

*Ps. cxxv, ii.

view. He passes a number of modern houses, built without order or taste on the stony, colourless upland. He then passes the ambitious structures of Russia,—a consulate, convent, and church; and then he gets a close view of the serried line of Saracenic walls, pierced in the centre before him by the deeply-recessed and picturesque Hebron or Joppa Gate (for it gets both names). Behind it, within, are the massive towers of the citadel.

He naturally looks for the Mount of Olives, which, above all other hills, has fixed itself in his mind; and perhaps, in reply to an eager question, the guide points to a gray, wavy line beyond the city, and scarcely overtopping the buildings. Though a mile distant, the air is so

HEBRON OR JOPPA GATE.

transparent and the colouring so uniform that it seems close at hand. Then, besides, it has no striking features,—in fact, it may be said to have no features at all. Yet this is Olivet, one of the grandest centres of sacred and historic associations. Photographs in an Eastern climate show those artistic defects somewhat too clearly, and consequently they are generally flat and uninteresting. I have seen many sketches, but, as a rule, the imagination of the artist has exaggerated both the apparent distance and the elevations, and thus truth is sacrificed to effect. The view given on preceding page, photographed from a commanding point on Zion near the Pool of Hezekiah, is an accurate picture of the ridge of Olivet. Another view, taken from the gardens on the southern slope of Moriah, outside the Haram area, shows a section of the ridge of Olivet, south of the former, with the Church of the Ascension and the adjoining convent. The irregular walls in the foreground are those of the more modern city, where they abut on the great wall of the Haram. The beautiful dome high up on the left is the Mosque el-Aksa.

Haram Wall.　　Mosque el-Aksa.　　Olivet, and Church of the Ascension.

THE MOSQUE EL-AKSA (SOUTH SIDE).
(*With Wall of Haram, and City Wall.*)

JERUSALEM FROM THE NORTH.

THE view of Jerusalem from the north is more picturesque and somewhat more interesting than that from the west. The ridge of Scopus, a western prolongation of Olivet, where the Roman emperor Titus is said to have encamped ere he descended to the final and fatal siege, affords a good panoramic prospect. Immediately below it, in the shallow head of the Kidron, is a remarkable group of rock-hewn tombs; one of them, the so-called Tomb of the Kings, is the grandest about Jerusalem. Beyond it is an undulating expanse of corn-fields, vineyards, and olive-groves, once covered with buildings. Beyond these again are the walls, over which appear the domes of the Church of the Sepulchre, and the new Jewish Synagogue, and the Tower of David, on Zion. A little to the left is the beautiful dome of the Great Mosque, on the site of the Temple; farther to the left still is the long valley of the Kidron, with the city wall on its western brow and the whole ridge of Olivet running along its eastern side. In its centre stands alone the pillar of Absalom's Tomb.

VIEW FROM OLIVET.

IF the views from the west and north are somewhat disappointing to the ardent, imaginative pilgrim, that from Olivet dispels all feelings of disappointment, and completely entrances him. Such at least was my experience. I was specially favoured during my first visit; and I have had many opportunities of renewing my first deep impressions. An old and dear friend had rented a little tower high up on the western brow of the hill. It commands a noble view of the Holy City and the surrounding country from Bethlehem to Mizpeh. It is one of those rude, square, miniature towers, which in ancient as in modern times proprietors built in their vineyards as residences for keepers and store-houses for fruit and wine. Here I took up my quarters with my friend, and from open window or terraced roof, at all hours, day and night, I looked on that wondrous panorama. During the soft, ruddy morning twilight; in the full blaze of noonday; in the dead stillness of night, when the moon shed her silver rays on the white walls and roofs of the city, my eyes were upon it—never wearying, never satisfied—ever detecting some new beauty in tint or form, some fresh spot of sacred interest or historic renown. Two artist friends were occasionally with us. One of them, alas! is gone—Thomas Seddon. I frequently stood beside his easel, under the shade of an olive, on the precipitous bank near Aceldama, as he painted that remarkable picture of the Kidron, now in South Kensington, the gift of a few friends and admirers to the nation. While he sat and worked, the shepherd, in his "coat of many colours," lay on the ground before him, and the goats sported on every side. I marked the wondrous accuracy and marvellous pre-Raphaelite minuteness of detail with which he caught the hue of every flower and thistle, and figured every shrub and stone in the foreground, and every ruin, and tomb, and house, and tree, and crag, down in the ravine, and up by the village of Siloam and the Jewish cemetery, to the heights of Olivet. I have heard critics declare its colouring unnatural, and its

This page is adjacent to a plate and is intentionally left blank.

PANORAMA OF
FROM THE MOUNT

OF JERUSALEM
MOUNT OF OLIVES

This page is adjacent to a plate and is intentionally left blank.

details exaggerated; but had they seen the landscape as I saw it, under the full glow of a Syrian summer sun, in an atmosphere of crystal transparency, they could not have failed to acknowledge and admire its matchless truthfulness. Poor Seddon caught his fatal illness there by drinking the foul water of the well of En-Rogel, down in the bottom of the neighbouring glen of Tophet. The accompanying engraving gives the chief portion of Seddon's painting, with the little tower in which we spent happy evenings together, on the hill-top in the distance.

The other artist with whom we had pleasant intercourse still lives, ennobling by his brilliant

LOWER VALLEY OF JEHOSHAPHAT, OR KIDRON.
(*With the Village of Siloam, and King's Garden.*)

genius and splendid works the art of our country. Holman Hunt was engaged on a painting, now of world-wide fame, "The Finding of Christ in the Temple." The conclave of Jewish rabbis, sitting there in mute astonishment before the Divine Boy, are all of them life-portraits, painted on the spot. In one of them I easily recognize my Jewish guide, who took me through many a lane and into many a house among his people on Mount Zion.

I trust Holman Hunt, should he ever chance to see these lines, will, with characteristic courtesy, pardon this passing allusion. The incident is among the brightest in my long Eastern wanderings. While I live I can never forget the views I there gained of Jerusalem from the Mount of Olives.

But I must now return to the details of that first visit. Morning dawned, and with my genial host, to whom every spot in and around Jerusalem was familiar, I went up to the terraced roof. Behind Olivet, on the east, the sky was all aglow with red light, which shot slanting across the hill-tops and projecting cliffs, and upon the walls and higher buildings of the city, throwing them up in bold relief from the darkly-shaded glens. No time could have been more favourable, no spot better fitted for seeing and studying the general contour and features of Jerusalem. The entire site was before me, distinct as an embossed map. At my feet, along the base of Olivet, ran the Kidron valley, deep and narrow, winding down from the undulating table-land on the north, and disappearing behind the shoulder of Olivet, and the rock-hewn houses of Siloam on the south—its banks clothed with terraced vineyards and dotted all over with olives; and down deep in its bed, at my feet, the venerable trees of Gethsemane.

Directly in front of me, on the other side of the Kidron, was Moriah, its bare shingly side rising precipitously from the bottom of the valley to a height of two hundred feet or more; and on its summit, supported by a colossal wall, the great rectangular platform of the old Temple and modern Haram. It is encompassed and supported by that wall, founded probably by Solomon, in places eighty feet high, and looking even higher where it impends over the ravine. This platform is the most striking feature of the city. It is about thirty acres in extent, and is studded with buildings of great beauty. On the whole, there is perhaps nothing like it in the world. I have seen the platform of the Temple of the Sun at Palmyra; I have seen the Stylobate of Baalbek; and I have seen the Acropolis of Athens; but the Temple platform of Jerusalem is grander than any of them. The accompanying engravings, from photographs, give some idea of its extent and general aspect. That taken from the Church of St. Anne on the north, recently restored by the French, shows most of the buildings. In the immediate foreground is the church; behind it the dark northern wall of the Haram area; on the right the terraced roofs of the houses of Zion.

The Haram area is an artificial platform on the top of Moriah, sustained on all sides by walls of great strength and vast antiquity. Its history is wonderful. It has been a holy place for well-nigh thirty centuries—from that time when David saw "the angel of the Lord stand between the earth and the heaven," over "the threshing-floor of Ornan the Jebusite," and "built there an altar unto the Lord."* Perhaps it may have been on the same spot Abraham offered the ram instead of his son. Be this as it may, on it the Temple was built, in whose shrine the glory of the Lord so often appeared, and in whose courts the Son of God so often taught. On it now stands the Great Mosque, called, from the bare rocky crown of Moriah within it, *The Dome of the Rock*. It is, and has been for twelve centuries, *The Noble Sanctuary* of the Muslems—next to Mecca,

---

* 1 Chron. xxi. 16-26.

VIEW OF THE HARAM AREA FROM BESIDE THE CHURCH OF ST. ANNE.

El-Aksa.   Mosque of Omar.   Jewish Synagogue.   Mount Zion.

This page is adjacent to a plate and is intentionally left blank.

their most venerated shrine. The platform itself, simple and massive, is grand and striking; but the buildings add greatly to its beauty. In the centre, on a raised platform of white marble, is the octagonal mosque, incrusted with encaustic tiles of gorgeous colours, and surmounted by a graceful dome. From the platform the ground slopes to the cloisters on the encircling ramparts, in gentle undulations of green turf, ornamented with marble arcades, gilded cupolas, fountains, and prayer-niches. At the southern end is the Mosque el-Aksa, formerly the Church of the Virgin. The quiet seclusion of the Haram, the rich green of its grass and foliage, the dazzling whiteness of its pavements and fountains, the brilliant tints of the central mosque, and, above all, its sacred associations, which even Muslim fanaticism and blasphemy cannot destroy, make it one of the most charming and interesting spots on earth.

Just behind the Haram the Tyropœon Valley can be traced from Olivet by a darkly shaded belt, running through the city from north to south. Beyond it is Zion, higher than Moriah—the confused mass of terraced roofs and cupolas rising up to the white buildings and domes of the Jewish synagogue and Armenian convent. The southern section of Mount Zion is now outside the city, covered with gardens and fields. As I looked at them from Olivet, I observed a moving object, and turning my glass to the spot, I saw a plough and yoke of oxen at work. Jeremiah's prophecy is fulfilled to the letter—"Zion shall be ploughed like a field."*

When I stood that first morning of my visit on the flat roof of the little tower, up on the western brow of Olivet, and looked down upon the Holy City crowning those battlemented heights, encircled by those deep dark ravines, I involuntarily said to my companion, "Beautiful for situation, the joy of the whole earth, is mount Zion…the city of the great King."† And as I stood and looked, the red rays of the rising sun shed a golden halo round the top of the Castle of David; then they tipped with gold each crescent-topped minaret, each dome of mosque and church and synagogue; and at length bathed in one flood of ruddy light the terraced roofs of the city, the grass and foliage, the cupolas, pavements, and colossal sustaining walls of the Haram. No human being could be disappointed who first saw Jerusalem, as I did, from the Mount of Olives.

*Jer. xxvi. 18.   †Ps. xlviii. 2.

WALK ROUND THE WALLS.

IN the eastern wall there is but one open gate. Some call it St. Stephen's Gate, from a fifteenth century tradition that the first Christian martyr was stoned a few yards outside it, close to the path leading down to Gethsemane. Others called it the Gate of our Lady Mary, and there is a large reservoir not far distant bearing the name of the Virgin. All the roads from Olivet, Bethany, and Jericho meet here, and from this spot we commence our walk. It is a plain Saracenic portal, with pointed arch above and a depressed one beneath. On each side of the upper arch are rudely sculptured lions, as may be seen on the accompanying engraving.

ST. STEPHEN'S GATE.

Instead of entering, we turn to the left, and walking along the side of the wall, soon reach the square tower at the north-east angle of the Haram. The enormous size of the stones in the lower courses of the masonry—some of them being more than twenty-four feet long—and the peculiar moulding of their edges, seem to prove that the building was erected not later, and probably much earlier, than the time of Herod the Great. It was one of the external towers of the fortress of Antonia, which defended the Temple on the north. In it the Roman garrison was quartered, and in it was Pilate's "Judgment Hall," where our Lord was condemned.*

The excavations of the Palestine Exploration Fund have shown that the foundations of the tower were laid upon the rock, at a depth of a hundred feet beneath the present surface of the ground. The whole of that vast depth has been filled up with

*Matt. xxviii. 19.

ruins. It is most interesting to note that Phœnician letters in red paint, evidently masons' marks, were found on several of the great foundation-stones. Does not this remind us of the historic record in 1 Kings v. 17 regarding the building of Solomon's Temple? The Jews were not skilled

THE GOLDEN GATE—EXTERIOR VIEW.

in architecture, but the Phœnicians were. So Solomon asked Hiram, king of Tyre, to send him workmen. He consented; and we read that "they hewed out great stones, costly stones, to lay the foundations of the house with wrought stone. And Solomon's builders and Hiram's builders and the Gebalites did fashion them." The Gebalites were inhabitants of the Phœnician city of Gebal, at the base of Lebanon. May not these and others, to which I shall refer presently, be the marks of those very masons?

The *Golden Gate*, now shut up, is one of the most striking features of the eastern wall of the Haram; but the close observer can easily see that it has been inserted at a comparatively recent period. The debased Corinthian capitals that support the florid entablature of the double arch, bear no resemblance in style to the massive simplicity of the masonry on each side. The architecture of the interior towards the Haram is peculiar, having Corinthian and Ionic columns, with exaggerated capitals, supporting a groined roof. It may have been inserted about the time

TOMBS IN THE VALLEY OF JEHOSHAPHAT.
(*With the Jewish Cemetery, and Mount of Olives.*)

of Constantine, evidently, however, on the site of an older gate, the colossal monolithic jambs of which remain, and may be seen from the inside.

We continue our walk southward at the base of the wall, among the quaint tombs of the Muslem Cemetery, shown in the engraving at page 11. The masonry here is irregular. Some of the stones are large and ancient, but the upper portion is modern. Here and there fragments of columns—granite, porphyry, and verd-antique—may be noticed in it. One near the top projects several feet, and has a singular tradition attached to it. On this, say Muslem doctors, the Prophet will take his seat on the Day of Judgment to direct affairs in the valley below. That part of the tradition which locates the scene of the Judgment in this valley is borrowed from Jewish rabbis, and has its origin in a wrong interpretation of Joel iii. 12, where the prophet says: "Let the nations come up to the valley of Jehoshaphat: for there will I sit to judge all the nations." There is no allusion to the last great Day; but, be this as it may, the tradition exercises a powerful influence on both Muslems and Jews. The favourite burying-place of the former is here, close to the Haram wall, on the bank of the valley; and the poor Jews often travel with toil and much suffering from the ends of the earth, that they may lay their bones in the vast cemetery which covers the opposite side of the Kidron and the lower slopes of Olivet.

The Pinnacle of the Temple.—As we proceed southward along the wall, the ground becomes narrower, and at length there is barely room for the path. The south-eastern angle stands on the very edge of the ravine, and is in many respects one of the most interesting relics of ancient Jerusalem. The wall rises to a height of seventy feet above the present surface of the ground; and its lower and more ancient section consists of fourteen layers of bevelled or drafted stones, averaging about three feet six inches in height, and some of the corner-stones measure twenty feet in length. The excavations of the English engineers reached the foundation upon the rock at a depth of seventy-seven feet. The lower part is constructed of great stones, hewn quite smooth, and the edges drafted, so that the surface of the wall resembles panel-work. Phœnician letters are found on many of the stones in the lowest courses, some incised to the depth of nearly an inch, others painted in vermilion. The impression left on the engineers was that the letters were quarry marks, cut or painted on each stone before it was laid, perhaps to indicate the position for which it was hewn. The painted marks are very large, several as much as twelve inches high. Mr. Deutsch says of them: "They do not represent any inscription. They are Phœnician. I consider them to be partly letters, partly numerals, and partly special masons' or quarry signs. Some of them were recognizable at once as well-known Phœnician characters; others, hitherto unknown in Phœnician epigraphy, I had the rare satisfaction of being able to identify on undoubted Phœnician structures in Syria." How deeply interesting is all this in connection with the Bible narrative of the building of the Temple mentioned above, and also of the further record in 1 Kings vii. 10: "And the foundation was of costly stones, even great stones, stones of ten cubits, and stones of eight cubits!" The Jewish architects, taught by their Phœnician neighbours, bestowed special care upon the corners of their great buildings. They show a finish, a solidity and choice of material, superior to other parts. Their "chief corner-stones," as seen here, are of fine proportions and surpassing magnitude. Does not this illustrate the well-known words of Isaiah: "Behold, I lay in Zion for a foundation a stone, a tried stone, a precious corner-stone of sure foundation"?* And how beautifully expressive is the

---

*Isa. xxviii 16.

language of the Psalmist: "Our daughters are corner-stones, polished after the similitude of a palace"!* One of the corner-stones of this angle weighs over one hundred tons.

The angle, as I have shown, springs from the very brow of the ravine. The lowest stone is partly embedded in the rock, on the top of a cliff. And we read, in the history of Josephus, that in Herod's time a lofty tower stood on top of the angle, uniting the Royal Cloisters, which ran along the southern end of the Temple area, with the cloisters, or "Porch of Solomon,"† which ran along the eastern side. Josephus thus describes the tower, and its enormous height above the bottom of the Kidron: "If any one looked from the top of the battlements down both those

WALL AT THE SOUTH-EAST ANGLE OF THE HARAM AREA.
(*Site of Pinnacle of the Temple.*)

altitudes, he would fell giddy, while his sight could not reach to such an immense depth." This is doubtless that "pinnacle of the Temple" mentioned by the evangelist in the temptation of our Lord.‡ "Then the devil taketh him into the holy city; and he set him on the pinnacle of the temple, and saith, If thou art the Son of God, cast thyself down," etc. The entire height, from the summit of the corner tower to the bottom of the ravine below, could not have been less than three hundred feet.

The accompanying engraving of the south side of the angle, looking towards Olivet

---

*Ps. cxliv. 12.   †John x. 23.   ‡Matt. iv.

over the Kidron, gives a good idea of the present aspect of the masonry. Beautiful architectural views of this angle, with copies of the Phœnician characters, full size, may be seen in the great work of the Palestine Exploration Fund, which is a perfect store-house of everything bearing upon the monuments of Jerusalem and the Holy Land.

South Wall of Haram, and Ophel.—We turn round the Pinnacle of the Temple, and proceed westward along the side of the great wall, having the hill *Ophel* on our left. It is a southern extension of Moriah, reaching down, with the Kidron on one side and the Tyropœon on the other, to that broader section of the former usually called the "King's Dale," the traditional scene of the meeting of Abram and Melchizedek,* and the reputed site of Absalom's Tomb.† The top of Ophel is broad, and descends rapidly, in terraces of little corn-fields and vineyards, to a cliff overhanging the Pool of Siloam. Ophel was made a suburb of Jerusalem in the time of Jotham;‡ and after the captivity it was inhabited chiefly by the Temple servants.§ Recent excavations laid bare a section of its ancient wall and the private entrances of the priests to the Temple.

In passing along, we notice a gateway with pointed arch. It is now walled up, but it formerly opened into a vast series of vaults beneath the Haram, usually called Solomon's Stables. Further on is a triple gate with round arches, also walled up. It led into the same vaults. These, and another opening some twenty feet below them, may have been intended as private passages for the entrance of the Temple servants.

Double Gate.—At the place where the Saracenic city wall joins, at right angles, the great wall of the Haram, is one of the most interesting gates of the Temple area. The exterior is now to a large extent covered with the city wall; but through a small grated window one is able to get a dim view of a long subterranean avenue, leading up an inclined plane and flight of steps to the Haram. When last in Jerusalem I was permitted to visit and inspect the whole interior of this most remarkable passage, which was apparently intended for the priests and officers of the Temple.

The gate is double, forty-two feet wide, and evidently ancient. It is divided in the centre by a massive rectangular pier, with small modern columns attached, as seen in the accompanying engraving. Within the gate is a hall, sixty-three feet long, and the width of the gate. In the centre is a huge monolithic column, twenty-one feet high, and nearly seven in diameter. The capital has a perpendicular palm-leaf ornament, which, Mr. Fergusson says, is at least as old as the time of Herod. The roof is vaulted, of good workmanship, the flat arches springing from the central monolith and piers, and from pilasters at the sides. The entire masonry seemed to me to be of the oldest type, but

*Gen. xiv. 17.   †2 Sam. xviii. 18.   ‡2 Chron. xxviii. 3.   §Neh. iii. 26.

chiselled and re-formed externally in Roman times. Some of the stones are thirteen feet long. The passage ascends gradually, and at the distance of about two hundred and sixty feet from the gate, opens out on the Haram area, in front of the Mosque el-Aksa.

Recent explorations show that there is a similar passage leading up from the triple gate

PIER IN THE VAULTS OF THE MOSQUE EL-AKSA.

already mentioned to the Haram. These may probably be the Huldah Gates of the Talmud, and those referred to by Josephus in a somewhat obscure passage, in which he says that the southern side of the Temple area "had gates about the middle." One of the two is most likely the "water gate" mentioned by Nehemiah: "Now the Nethinim dwelt in Ophel, unto the place over against the water gate toward the east."* It is a

*Neh. iii. 26.

noteworthy fact that, at a depth of nineteen feet below the triple gate, a water-course was found, partly hewn in the rock, and apparently communicating with the cisterns under the Haram.

The more thorough and minute our examination of holy places, the more complete will be our illustration and our understanding of Holy Scripture.

PILLAR OF DOUBLE GATEWAY UNDER THE MOSQUE EL-AKSA.

The *South-West Angle* of the Haram resembles the south-east; but it is in some respects even more interesting. It is, perhaps, on the whole, one of the grandest specimens of ancient mural architecture in the world. The stones are larger than any we have hitherto met with. One corner-stone measures over thirty-eight feet in length by nearly four feet in height. They are much worn by time—perhaps also by the falling of ruins and rubbish. The excavations of the English engineers show that the southern wall of the Haram was built right across the bottom of the Tyropœon Valley, at a depth of ninety feet beneath the present surface of the ground; and the south-western angle was founded on the rock on the western side of the valley, at a depth of sixty feet. In one of the shafts sunk during the excavations a signet was found bearing an inscription in the oldest type of Hebrew letters, "Haggai, son of Shebna."

The accompanying picture gives a view of this angle, with a section of the western wall up to and beyond the abutment of the ancient bridge, and also of the buildings upon

JERUSALEM FROM MOUNT ZION—SOUTH-WEST ANGLE OF HARAM.

the Haram area, the Great Mosque being in the centre. Dense jungles of prickly-pear now fill the Tyropœon Valley, and extend far up the side of Zion on the left.

The Bridge.—One of the most interesting fragments of ancient architecture around the Haram area is the abutment of the bridge that once spanned the Tyropœon, connecting the Royal Palace on Zion with the Temple Court on Moriah. From without it is somewhat difficult of access. There is no gate in the city wall near the Haram, and in going from Ophel we must pass round the angle of the wall towards Zion, to a little postern, called the Gate of the Moors, which I found usually open on Fridays. Entering, we are in a wilderness of ruins and rubbish-heaps, overgrown with rank weeds and jungles of giant-cactus. The shattered and wretched-looking houses of the Jewish quarter cling to the precipitous side of their beloved Zion. A tortuous path, encumbered with filth, and noisome with the putrid remains of dead dogs, cats, and camels, winds through a scene of mournful desolation. As we pass along, the terrible prophetic words of Micah come up vividly to one's mind:—"Therefore shall Zion for your sake be plowed as a field, and Jerusalem shall become heaps, and the mountain of the house as the high places of the forest."* At length we reach the south-western angle of the Haram, and feel amply repaid for a toilsome and unpleasant walk.

JEWISH FAMILY IN MOUNT ZION.

Struggling on northward along the side of the wall, we observe, at a distance of about forty feet from the angle, three courses of colossal masonry projecting from the line of the wall, and forming the springing course of an arch. They were first observed by that eminent geographer and traveller, the late Dr. Robinson of New York; and they have since his time attracted no little attention, and given rise to no small amount of controversy. He, after careful thought and measurement, concluded that they formed part of the bridge which in early times connected Zion with the Temple. Recent excavations have put the fact beyond all question.

*Micah iii. 12.

Captain Warren discovered the first pier, directly opposite the springing course, forty-two feet distant from it, and at a depth of forty-two feet below the surface. Between the pier and the Haram wall he found the fallen stones of the arch. The arch was thus forty-two feet in span, and five such would be required to cross the valley. The bridge was fifty-one feet wide, and the

ROBINSON'S ARCH.

height of the roadway above the bottom of the ravine was not less than one hundred and twenty feet.

The bridge is first definitely mentioned during the siege of the city by Pompey, twenty years before Herod was made king. Josephus describes the house of the Asmonæan princes as being in the upper town, Zion, and states that a bridge connected the upper town with the Temple. That the bridge therefore existed in the days of our Lord

JEWS' WAILING-PLACE.

This page is adjacent to a plate and is intentionally left blank.

cannot be doubted. One thing is certain regarding the existing fragment,—it is coeval with the massive foundations of the southern angles of the Haram, and is thus of earlier date than the Temple of Herod.

Another fact of singular interest has been brought to light by the excavations of the English engineers. More than twenty feet below an old pavement on which the ruins of Robinson's arch lie, Captain Warren discovered the remains of a still older bridge. The bridge whose abutment is now seen in the Haram wall cannot be assigned to a later period than the reign of Herod; consequently, as I venture to think, the older bridge belonged either to the Second Temple or to the Temple of Solomon.

Solomon's Ascent to the Temple.—In three passages of Scripture a remarkable "ascent" or "causeway" is mentioned, leading from the Palace on Zion to the Temple, and specially designed for the use of the king.* May we not, with some degree of probability, identify this "ascent" with the viaduct which, according to Josephus, connected the Royal Palace on Zion with the Temple on Moriah? Such a monument of skill and power might well make a deep impression on the Queen of Sheba, and cause the proud Jewish historian to write these words:—"And when the queen of Sheba had seen all the wisdom of Solomon, and the house that he had built…and his ascent by which he went up unto the house of the Lord, there was no more spirit in her."

What a train of associations, sacred and historic, and what a crowd of feelings, joyous and sorrowful, do these few stones awaken! Over the noble bridge which they supported marched in solemn splendour the kings and princes of Israel to worship God in his Temple. Over it, too, humble and despised, often passed the Son of God himself, to carry a message of heavenly peace to a rebel world. Upon its shattered arch the victorious Titus once stood, and pointing to the burning Temple behind him, made a final appeal to the remnant of the Jews on Zion to lay down their arms and save themselves from slaughter by submission to Rome. Now, Temple, Bridge, and Palace are gone. Within the precincts of the Temple court no Jew dare set his foot; and on the site of the Royal Palace the wretched dwellings of that poor despised race are huddled together in misery and squalor.

The Place of Wailing.—Entering the inhabited part of the old city, and winding through some crooked filthy lanes, I suddenly found myself, on turning a sharp corner, in a spot of singular interest—the "Jews' Place of Wailing." It is a small paved quadrangle; on one side are the backs of low modern houses, without door or window; on the other is the lofty wall of the Haram, of recent date above, but having below five courses of bevelled stones in a good state of preservation. Here the Jews are permitted to approach the sacred inclosure, and wail over the fallen Temple, whose very dust is dear to them, and in

*1 Kings x. 5;   1 Chron. xxvi. 16;   2 Chron. ix. 3, 4.

whose stones they still take pleasure.* It was Friday, and a crowd of poor devotees had assembled-men and women of all ages and all nations, dressed in the quaint costumes of every country of Europe and Asia. Old men were there,—pale, haggard, careworn men, tottering on pilgrim staves; and little girls with white faces, and lustrous black eyes, gazing wistfully now at their parents, now at the old wall. Some were on their knees, chanting mournfully from a book of Hebrew prayers, swaying their bodies to and fro; some were prostrate on the ground, pressing forehead and lips to the earth; some were close to the wall, burying their faces in the rents and crannies of the old stones; some were kissing them, some had their arms spread out as if they would clasp them to their bosoms, some were bathing them with tears, and all the while sobbing as if their hearts would burst. It was a sad and touching spectacle. Eighteen centuries of exile and woe have not dulled their hearts' affections, or deadened their feelings of national devotion. Here we see them assembled from the ends of the earth, poor, despised, down-trodden outcasts, amid the desolations of their fatherland, beside the dishonoured ruins of their ancient sanctuary, chanting, now in accents of deep pathos, and now of wild woe, the prophetic words of their own Psalmist,—"*O God, the heathen are come into thine inheritance; thy holy temple have they defiled...We are become a reproach to our neighbours, a scorn and derision to them that are round about us. How long, Lord? wilt thou be angry for ever?*"†

> "Oh, weep for those that wept by Babel's stream,
> Whose shrines are desolate, whose land a dream;
> Weep for the harp of Judah's broken spell;
> Mourn—where their God hath dwelt, the godless dwell!"

On certain occasions, towards evening, the following litany is chanted. The accompanying engraving represents two Jews chanting.

    Leader: *For the palace that lies desolate*:—Response: *We sit in solitude and mourn*.

    L. *For the palace that is destroyed*:—R. *We sit*, etc.

    L. *For the walls that are overthrown*:—R. *We sit*, etc.

    L. *For our majesty that is departed*:—R. *We sit*, etc.

    L. *For our great men who lie dead*:—R. *We sit*, etc.

    L. *For the precious stones that are burned*:—R. *We sit*, etc.

    L. *For the priests who have stumbled*:—R. *We sit*, etc.

    L. *For our kings who have despised Him*:—R. *We sit*, etc.

Another antiphon is as follows:—

    Leader: *We pray Thee, have mercy on Zion!*—Response: *Gather the children of Jerusalem.*

    L. *Haste, haste, Redeemer of Zion!*—R. *Speak to the heart of Jerusalem.*

---

*Ps. cii. 14.   †Ps. lxxix. 1, 4, 5.

AT THE PLACE OF WAILING.

This page is adjacent to a plate and is intentionally left blank.

L. *May beauty and majesty surround Zion!*—R. *Ah! turn Thyself mercifully to Jerusalem.*

L. *May the kingdom soon return to Zion!*—R. *Comfort those who mourn over Jerusalem.*

L. *May peace and joy abide with Zion!*—R. *And the branch (of Jesse) spring up at Jerusalem.*

PILATE'S HOUSE, OVERLOOKING HARAM AREA.

THE TEMPLE AND ITS COURTS.

FOR well-nigh four thousand years Mount Moriah has been the most venerated spot in Jerusalem. It was the nucleus of all the holy places; and it has this advantage, that its identity cannot be disputed. From Melchizedek to David, from David to his greater Son, and down even to our own day, Jewish hearts have clung to Moriah, and the longing looks of the whole Jewish people have been fondly turned to it.

During my first visit to Jerusalem, the Temple area was sternly closed against *Kafers*—that is, non-Muslems of every sect and country. For Christian or Jew to enter was almost certain death. I tried to peep in through the open gates, but was rudely, even savagely, driven back by dervishes. As a last resource my kind companion took me to the palace of the pasha at the north-west angle. He had the *entrée*, and we were soon on the

REMAINS OF FORT ANTONIA, IN VIA DOLOROSA.

terraced roof which commands the whole area. The palace is historically interesting. It occupies part of the site of the fortress of Antonia. Nehemiah calls it "the castle which appertaineth to the house" (Temple). It was occupied by Pilate and his Roman garrison in the time of our Lord. The engraving on preceding page shows the side towards the Haram; and in the above cut we see some fragments of the ancient masonry in the Via

GENERAL VIEW OF THE MOSQUE OF OMAR.

This page is adjacent to a plate and is intentionally left blank.

Dolorosa on the opposite side of the house. From the flat roof one obtains perhaps the very best general view of the Haram and its numerous buildings. It nearly corresponds to the view from the Church of St. Anne already given.

The state of matters in Jerusalem has greatly changed since my first visit thirty years ago. Christian gold has conquered Muslem fanaticism. Free entrance to the Haram is now obtained by payment of a small fee. During my last visit I was particularly fortunate. A shrewd French engineer in the Turkish service had detected, or at least said he had detected, dangerous rents in the walls of the mosques, and grave defects in other parts. He informed the pasha that the venerable structures could only be saved from utter ruin by immediate and thorough repair. Of course the necessary order was issued, and the Christian engineer employed a large staff of workmen, mostly Christians; the work of repair and renovation was proceeding when I reached Jerusalem.

A letter from my old friend Consul Moore to the chief guardian of the Haram secured entrance, and the presence of the consul's gorgeously dressed janissary, coupled with a whisper to the guardian of additional *bakshish* from the party, made inspection easy. When I addressed the venerable Arab *mullah* in his own tongue, with a profusion of Oriental titles and compliments, the crowd of scowling dervishes and fawning fakirs who seemed intent on following us was at once dispersed. Of course the sacred buildings and precincts had already been polluted by the feet of Christian workmen, so we had no trouble about putting on slippers. In my riding-boots, note-book in hand, I visited every spot, had pointed out to me every holy shrine, and was told every strange tradition. The guardian seemed to delight in showing his vast erudition. This was just what I had often longed for, but had scarcely ventured to anticipate.

Our steps were naturally first turned to the central mosque. It is a perfect gem. I was much struck with the chasteness of design, and wonderful minuteness and delicacy of detail, in the Saracenic architecture. The encaustic tiles which cover the whole exterior reflect in gorgeous hues the bright sunlight. Over the windows and round the cornice are broad borders of beautifully interlaced Arabic characters, so large that one can easily read them from below. A graceful dome, tipped with a golden crescent, crowns the whole, and is seen from afar. The position of the mosque, raised on a platform of white marble, so as to overtop all other buildings, adds vastly to the appearance. It is octagonal in form, each side measuring sixty-seven feet. Four doors facing the cardinal points lead to the interior, which is one hundred and forty-eight feet in diameter, the dome being sixty-six. The principal door has a portico with small marble columns, as seen on the accompanying engraving. The plan of the interior is peculiar, and, so far as I know, unique. There are two concentric rings of columns and piers supporting the roof, leaving corridors, or aisles, between; the outer thirteen feet wide, the inner thirty. The columns are marble, but not of uniform size, and were evidently rifled from other buildings, as is almost invariably the case in the old mosques of Syria. It is lighted by fifty-six pointed windows, filled with stained glass of extraordinary brilliancy and beauty.

Directly under the dome is the shrine of the mosque and of the entire Haram. It is a bare rock, the natural crown of Moriah, about sixty feet across, and rising some six feet above the floor. It gives its name to the building—*Kubbet es-Sukhrah*, "The Dome of the Rock." The origin of the mosque, as given by Muslim authorities, is interesting. It is as follows. After taking the city, the Khalif Omar asked where the Jewish Temple stood. The Patriarch took him to this rock, then covered with ruins. Omar, with his own hands, helped to remove the rubbish, and gave orders for the erection of the mosque. It is further said that it was rebuilt in a style of greater splendour by Abd el-Melek, who covered it with plates of gold. During the temporary rule of the Crusaders it was converted into a church, and they called it "The Temple of the Lord."

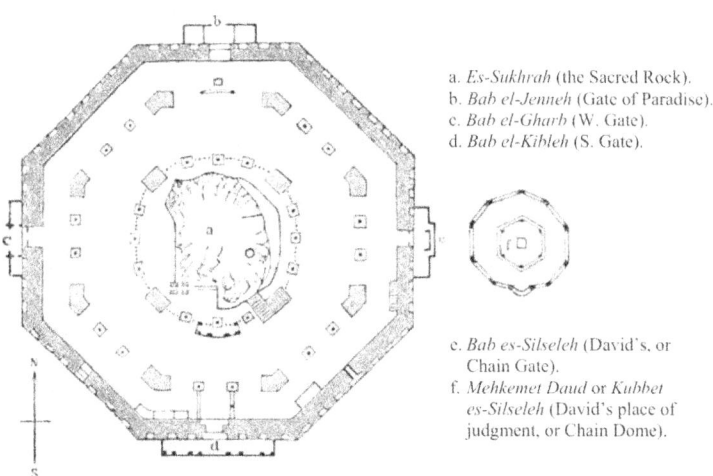

a. *Es-Sukhrah* (the Sacred Rock).
b. *Bab el-Jenneh* (Gate of Paradise).
c. *Bab el-Gharb* (W. Gate).
d. *Bab el-Kibleh* (S. Gate).
e. *Bab es-Silseleh* (David's, or Chain Gate).
f. *Mehkemet Daud* or *Kubbet es-Silseleh* (David's place of judgment, or Chain Dome).

The sacred rock itself is specially deserving of notice. On its south-east side a flight of steps leads down to an excavated chamber, or cave, about six feet high. Here the guardian took me to several small altars and niches, which, he said, were dedicated respectively to Abraham, David, Solomon, Elias, and Gabriel. In the roof is a circular hole, cut through the entire thickness of the rock, and in the floor beneath it is a marble slab covering a deep cavity, called "The Well of the Spirits." The guardian whispered to me that some learned men considered it to be the entrance to Paradise; others equally learned, the entrance to the opposite region; "but," he added, "Allah alone knows the truth."

Going up the stairs again, the guardian pointed out to me, on a corner of the sacred rock, the "footprint of Mohammed," impressed as he stepped upon it to mount his horse Barak when commencing his ride to Paradise; and not far distant the "hand-print of

A PORTICO OF THE MOSQUE OF OMAR.

This page is adjacent to a plate and is intentionally left blank.

Gabriel," who seized the rock and held it down by main force as it was in the act of rising to follow the prophet.

Most of these stories are childish; but some features of the rock itself are of much importance. The rock was undoubtedly the summit of Moriah, which originally formed the threshing-floor of Araunah the Jebusite, where King David offered up sacrifice to stay the plague, and which afterwards, during the Jewish period, was the site of the great altar of burnt-

PULPIT ON THE PLATFORM OF THE HARAM.

offering in front of the east gate of the Temple. The circular hole was for draining off the blood and water, and the cave below was the cesspool. Other drains have been discovered to let in an abundant supply of water for cleansing purposes, and to sweep all away through the rocky hill-side down into the Kidron far below.

Site of the Temple.—We can now fix with almost absolute certainty the site of Solomon's Temple. It stood to the west of the altar of burnt-offering-that is, of the sacred rock. The altar, we read in the Talmud, was thirty-two cubits square, and thus covered nearly the whole space within the mosque. The east door of the Temple was near it, and the inner court, reserved for the priests, contained both the altar and the Temple, and may have embraced that section of the raised platform on the western side of the mosque.

But the Temple is gone. Not a stone, not a trace, remains. We can here again see with our eyes the judgment our Lord pronounced against Jerusalem literally executed. We look up to that beautiful pulpit where, on Fridays and festivals, the Muslem priests proclaim, in tones of high excitement, praise to Allah and his prophet, and death to all infidels, and we reflect how wonderfully time has changed the prophetic words of Ezekiel into historic facts: "I will bring the worst of the heathen, and they shall possess their houses…and their holy places shall be defiled."* And when we have on each side of us the forms of devotees prostrate in prayer before the shrine of the false prophet, we can sympathize with the poor Jews who look across

MUSLEM PRAYING.

the Tyropœon from their squalid dwellings upon Mount Zion, and cry in the touching words of the poet—

"Our Temple hath not left one stone,
And mockery sits on Salem's throne."

There are many other smaller buildings round the Great Mosque, rich in decoration and exquisite in taste. Mohammedans excel in ornamenting cupolas, niches, and fountains. Their carving; their open work in stone, marble, and wood; their interlaced inscription; their stalactite arches and corbals; their gilt ceilings; and their mosaic walls and pavements, are chaste in design and gorgeous in effect. Witness the Alhambra of Granada, and the Alkazar in Seville. Among those most worthy of note in the Haram

---

*Ezek. vii. 24.

PORCH OF THE MOSQUE EL-AKSA.

This page is adjacent to a plate and is intentionally left blank.

are the Dome of Solomon, near the northern end, the traditional spot where he offered up the prayer of dedication; the Dome of the Chain, where it is said David sat to give judgment—it is on the east side of the Great Mosque, and almost a *facsimile* of it in miniature; and the Dome of Elias. Most of them are seen on the accompanying engravings. Then again, the arcades which surround the raised platform—so slender, so beautiful in design, so striking in outline—are perhaps among the most characteristic examples of pure Saracenic workmanship. The section figured above, with the pulpit, is particularly worthy of notice.

Mosque el-Aksa.—Next to the Dome of the Rock, the Mosque el-Aksa is the largest and finest building in the Haram. It is at the south end, overhanging the Wall of Ophel, and its fine dome is conspicuous throughout the whole region southward as far as Bethlehem. Originally it was a church. About the middle of the sixth century the Emperor Justinian built a basilica in honour of the Virgin on this spot. It was taken by the Muslems and converted into a mosque. A century and a half later it was, to a large extent, rebuilt and much enlarged by El-Mahdi, the third Khalif of the Abassides. The Crusaders, of course, dedicated it to Christian worship, under the strange

DOME OF ELIAS IN THE HARAM AREA.

name of the Temple of Solomon and a portion of it was assigned to the new military order, *The Knights Templars*.

The porch is doubtless the work of the Templars. The interior is a basilica of seven aisles, and covers as much space as some of our great cathedrals. The architecture is mixed, and by no means chaste. There are Corinthian columns of white marble, and heavy Byzantine piers, with basket-shaped capitals. The arches are mostly pointed, but of different elevations. Some of the windows have richly-coloured glass, not equal in brilliancy, however, to those of the Dome of the Rock. Near the entrance is a magnificent wooden pulpit, made in Damascus, and brought to Jerusalem by Saladin. The intricate arabesques of its small raised panels are exquisitely carved. Just within the great door is a well, to which a singular tradition is attached. Mohammed said on one occasion that a faithful follower of his would enter Paradise walking. It so happened that in the days of Omar a number of the faithful came to Jerusalem to pray at the shrine of the Sacred Rock. One of them went to this well to draw water. His bucket fell to the bottom, and on going down to get it, to his great surprise he found an open door admitting to delightful gardens. He entered, walked through them, admiring their rare trees and flowers, and enjoying the delights of the wondrous bowers and sparkling fountains. On leaving he plucked a leaf, and stuck it, in Arab style, behind his ear. The story was reported to the governor of the city, who sent his servants with the stranger pilgrim to see the gardens; but no gardens and no door could now be found. The story was called in question, and as proof of the reality of his tale the pilgrim produced the leaf he had plucked. Omar was written to, and at once confirmed the truth of the statement, and said that the prediction of the prophet was now fulfilled: one of his followers had entered Paradise on his feet. To test the matter and confound doubters, he told them to examine the leaf. If it remained green, the story was true; there could be no doubt it was plucked in Paradise. The leaf of course preserved its verdure, and from that day the well has been called "The Well of the Leaf."

CLOISTERS AND PORCHES OF THE TEMPLE.

THE Temple had three courts. The first, "The Court of the Priests," included the Temple itself, or shrine, and the altar of burnt-offering. It was reserved for the priests and their immediate attendants. The second, called "The Inner Court," surrounded it, and was enclosed by a high ornamental wall or balustrade, on which, at intervals, were inscribed tablets in several languages, directing that no stranger, on pain of death, should enter. One of the tablets was discovered amid ruins a few years ago. This illustrates the incident recorded in the Acts of the Apostles, where we read that St. Paul was accused of having brought "Greeks into the temple, and defiled the holy place,"* and the people were therefore about to kill him. The third, or outer court, was open to all, and hence called "The Court of the Gentiles." It was, in fact, a public park to Jerusalem, where the people met, conversed, and even

---

*Acts xxi. 28.

SELLER OF BRACELETS IN COURT OF CHURCH OF THE HOLY SEPULCHRE.

This page is adjacent to a plate and is intentionally left blank.

bought and sold those articles required for the proper observance of festivals. From this court our Lord drove the dealers and money-changers; not so much apparently because the traffic was in itself unlawful, as because the priests who farmed it made it a source of dishonest gain. This seems to be indicated by the stinging reproof of our Lord: "It is written, My house shall be called a house of prayer; but ye make it a den of robbers."*

The New Testament writers draw a distinction between the Temple itself and the courts. The distinction is unfortunately not seen in our English version, but is very clear in the original Greek.

CHRISTIAN OIL-SELLERS.

The Temple is uniformly called *naos*, "the shrine," while the word *hieron* is used to signify the courts or "sacred inclosure." Our Lord drove the dealers out of the court, not out of the Temple itself, which they could not have entered. One sees something analogous at the present time in the courts of the Christian churches of Jerusalem and Bethany. Dealers in carved shells, crosses, beads, and even oil for lamps, sell their wares freely and continually in the courts of the Church of the Sepulchre and Church of the Nativity. The accompanying picture is a vivid representation

*Matt. xxi. 13.

of a seller of bracelets. In the other engraving is a group of three oil-sellers, with the jars and bottles, large and small, of native pottery; and hanging up, two plaited trays of straw for fruit.

The most magnificent buildings in the court of Herod's Temple were the "porches" or cloisters—covered avenues that extended along the sides. That on the south side was triple, with four ranges of white marble Corinthian columns, some of which may now be seen in the mosques. The central avenue is said to have been fifty feet wide and one hundred high; each side avenue was thirty feet wide and fifty high. The central avenue was exactly opposite the great bridge which crossed the Tyropœon from the Palace on Zion to the Temple area, and thus formed a grand entrance for royalty to the Temple court. It was called the Royal Porch, and was worthy of the name. The cloister on the eastern side had a double avenue, with three rows of columns, extending from the Royal Porch to the Tower of Antonia on the north. The shafts of all the columns, we are told, were monoliths of white marble, and the roofs overhead were of cedar, exquisitely carved and gilt. Considering the extent and splendour of the buildings, we cannot wonder at the statement by the Jews: "Forty and six years was this temple in building;"[*] nor can we wonder at the feeling of national pride which prompted the disciples of our Lord to say to him as they stood upon the brow of Olivet with the whole before them: "Master, behold what manner of stones and what manner of buildings!"[†]

The eastern cloister was called "Solomon's Porch;" and in it, as St. John tells us, our Lord was accustomed to walk, and doubtless to teach, after the manner, outwardly at least, of the Stoic philosophers of Greece.[‡] He also taught in that part of the inner court which, adjoined the treasury, and which was specially frequented by women. It was in Solomon's Porch the people crowded round Peter and John after they had cured the poor cripple at the gate "of the temple which is called Beautiful."[§]

The Pinnacle of the Temple, as I have already explained, was the lofty tower which stood on the angle of the encircling wall at the junction of the two porches. (See engraving, page 30.)

This plan of having temples encircled by spacious cloistered courts was not uncommon in the East. It was suitable for purposes of teaching, for discussions on religious and political subjects, and for popular assemblies. The Temple of the Sun at Palmyra has a court almost as large as that of Jerusalem, and surrounded on all sides by cloisters formed by a double row of columns, about one hundred of which still stand. The general effect is very grand. The Temple of Rimmon in Damascus, for a time a church, now a mosque, had also an open court surrounded by colonnades. The Temple of the Sun in Baalbek has a spacious open court, but instead of cloisters it has richly-ornamented side

---

[*] John ii. 20.   [†] Mark xiii. 1.   [‡] John x. 23; cf. viii. 20.   [§] Acts iii. 2-11.

recesses and chambers. The Greeks had their *stoas*; and the Acropolis of Athens reminds one, in many respects, of the Temple Mount in Jerusalem. Utility was in every instance combined with elegance and splendour. The instruction of the people in divine philosophy was not considered inconsistent with the cultivation of the taste and the promotion of high art. Man was taught in Jerusalem to dedicate to the service of God every faculty and gift with which God had endowed him—his inherent genius, his learning, his taste, his acquired skill, his wealth, his political power—in a word, everything he possessed.

Some will doubtless think it strange that a building of such great solidity and beauty as Herod's Temple should have disappeared from the top of Mount Moriah, and that not even a single stone or trace of it should now remain. None of the great temples of Greece or Rome, none of the famous temples of Syria, so far as I know, have been so utterly swept away. The country is studded with ruins, many of them much older than the time of Herod; yet the Temple of Jerusalem—the *naos*, the shrine, around which so many hallowed memories cluster,—"hath not left one stone."

History records, if not the reason, at least the fact. When Titus captured Jerusalem, we are told he left the city a mass of ruins. The acropolis of Antonia was razed to the ground to obtain more space for the mounds erected against the Temple, which was at length taken and burned. About fifty years afterwards the Emperor Hadrian built on the spot a temple of Jupiter, and set up an equestrian statue of himself on the very place known to the Jews as the "Holy of Holies." The statue was standing in the time of Jerome, towards the close of the fourth century. It was completely demolished by the Mohammedans, and, as I have already stated, the entire site was cleared by command of Omar, and the Great Mosque built.

WALLS AND GATES OF THE CITY.

THE Haram forms a separate quarter, entirely distinct from the city proper. We have passed round it from St. Stephen's Gate, and have examined the principal buildings and objects of interest in the interior. We now return to Zion.

About one-half of Mount Zion lies outside the city wall. Most of it is cultivated in terraced corn-fields and vineyards, breaking down abruptly into the valley of Hinnom on the south and the Tyropœon on the east. The summit of the hill is three hundred feet higher than the bottom of Hinnom and five hundred feet higher than En-Rogel at the junction of Hinnom and the Kidron. It is higher than any part of the present city.

Zion was the first spot in Jerusalem occupied by buildings. At a very early period the warlike tribes saw its advantageous position as a stronghold. The Jebusites fortified it, and for centuries defied the Israelites. "The children of Judah could not drive them out."* They even ventured to mock David and his shepherd warriors. But his followers, accustomed to climb the cliffs of En-gedi, scaled the heights of Zion, which thenceforth became the stronghold of Israel. Upon it David built his palace, and there for a thousand years the kings, his successors, reigned. One of the oldest towers of the present citadel bears David's name. (See engraving, p. 14.) Zion was the last spot in the city that held out against the Romans. When the rest of Jerusalem was in ruins, when the enemy occupied the courts of the Temple, the remnant of the Jews from the walls of Zion resolutely but vainly refused the terms of the conqueror, and perished around and within the palace of their kings.

ZION GATE.

The city which stood on Zion bore in succession many names. It was *Salem* of Melchizedek;† the *Jebus* of the Jebusites;‡ the *City of David*;§ the *Castle of Zion*;** and *Jerusalem*.¶ Josephus calls it the *Upper City*, and the *Upper Market*.

Zion Gate, called by the natives the *Gate of the Prophet David*, is a plain Saracenic portal, with a pointed arch above and a squaretopped door below it. On each side is an ornamental niche. Inside the gate is some unoccupied ground, and here one encounters the most painful sight in the whole city—a few poor dilapidated huts, occupied solely by lepers. They squat in the dust inside the gate, begging piteously from all who pass in and out; their voices husky; their features so disfigured by blotches and swellings as to be almost undistinguishable; their fingers, toes, hands, and feet in many cases eaten away. This seems to be the only place in Jerusalem where their presence is tolerated, and the inhabitants studiously avoid it. I have seen the lepers in Damascus in their

---

*Joshua xv. 63. †Gen. xiv. 18. ‡1 Chron. xi. 4. §2 Sam. v. 9. **Chron. xi. 5. ¶Joshua xviii. 20.

WALLS AND GATES OF THE CITY.

hospital, the traditional house of Naaman. I think the disease is not the true leprosy mentioned and minutely described in the Bible. It is incurable, but not infectious. It appears to be hereditary, and prevails only in certain districts. It is known to medical men as *elephantiasis*, and is one of the most loathsome forms of disease. The chief, or sheikh, of the lepers is here represented.

Leaving Zion Gate, it is interesting to walk along the side of the city wall, and to look down into the Valley of Hinnom on the left, a section of which has been converted into a great tank, called the Pool of the Sultan. Some consider this to be the "lower pool" mentioned by the prophet Isaiah,* and suppose that it was supplied with water from the fountain of Gihon, the outflow of which Hezekiah stopped "and brought it down to the west side of the city of David."† A little distance below the pool the aqueduct which originally brought water from Solomon's pools, beyond Bethlehem, to the cisterns in the Temple area, is seen crossing the valley.

SHEIKH OF THE LEPERS.

We now proceed past the Hebron or Jaffa Gate, already described (see page 16), and walk on northward between the city wall and the new Russian buildings. We soon reach the remains of a tower in the angle of the wall, constructed of massive stones of Jewish type. This seems to have been one of the towers of the second wall mentioned by Josephus as encircling Akra, a suburb or section of the city lying immediately north of Zion. From the tower the wall runs in a zigzag line over uneven ground to the depression along which the great northern road approaches the city. Here is the

Damascus Gate, one of the most picturesque of the city gates. The portal itself resembles that of Zion; but the battlements and projecting towers and machicolations give it an interesting and even formidable aspect. In its present state it is new. Even a cursory examination, however, reveals traces of ancient masonry deserving of

*Isa. xxii. 9.   †2 Chron. xxxii. 30.

special notice, and well worthy of the attention of every traveller. Just within the gate, on the east, are large hewn stones. Passing round these, we come to a square chamber adjoining the wall, whose sides are composed of bevelled stones similar to those in the exterior wall of the Haram. On the western side of the gate is a corresponding chamber. Some of the stones measure seven feet by nearly four, and appear to occupy their original places. Outside the gate, in the foundations of the wall, are similar stones. These are doubtless the remains of the Jewish

THE DAMASCUS GATE.

wall which surrounded Akra, and the chambers are guard-rooms of the old gate. Here sat the soldiers of the Asmonæan princes; and the wall and chambers may have been part of the work of the Jews under Nehemiah, when he repaired the broken walls and set up the gates.

Major Wilson's note on the Damascus Gate is interesting: "There is a large accumulation of rubbish in the neighbourhood of the gate, almost concealing the remains of an old entrance, over which the present one is built….The old arch is semicircular, and built of large plainly-chiselled stones; and from its appearance and position would seem to be of great age." Still more recent excavations have brought to light foundations of massive walls and of a tower. It was here the Romans made their first attack on the city; and the ruins now seen are, in all probability, those battered down by the Roman engines.

HOUSE OF DIVES.

This page is adjacent to a plate and is intentionally left blank.

A short distance outside the gate is a cave, called the *Grotto of Jeremiah*. It seems to be part of an old quarry, used for a time as a reservoir. Outside the wall, east of the gate, are deep cuttings in the rock, as if intended for a moat. Passing these, we reach the north-east angle, where the wall turns sharply southward near the brow of the Kidron valley, and runs along it to St. Stephen's Gate, close to the corner of the Haram.

WALK THROUGH THE CITY.

WE enter by St. Stephen's Gate, to wander through the streets of the holiest city in the world. My first impression was one of bitter disappointment. The streets are narrow, crooked, filthy. The houses are generally poor and dilapidated. There is no air of departed grandeur. There are no traces of architectural beauty and taste, such as one sees in Rome or Athens—such as one admires in Tyre and Damascus, Palmyra and Bozrah, and many another famous city of Syria. Instead of these our feelings are shocked and our common-sense outraged by apocryphal holy places, and by Scriptural names attached to buildings not three centuries old.

VIA DOLOROSA.

Just inside the gate we look into the so-called Pool of Bethesda, evidently a portion of the great moat which bounded and protected the fortress of Antonia on the north. We then enter the *Via Dolorosa*, a narrow lane running in a zigzag line from the House of Pilate to Calvary. A few of the reputed stations and traditional houses I shall mention as we pass rapidly along. Here is the gate of the Judgment Hall of Pilate, with a Saracenic arch. There is the House of Dives, without a trace of ancient glory about its Turkish windows and Arab domes. We may make short excursions to the right and left to get a fuller view of the city, or to visit objects of interest. Not far distant is the Church of St. Anne, a chaste building of the Crusading age, given some years ago to the French, and now restored in good taste. Near it is a French convent, and from the roof may be obtained a good view of the city, including the Haram and the whole buildings of Zion. When last there I was most courteously received by an English lady of high family, then a *religieuse*, who had devoted herself with rare zeal and self-denial to the work of education. I was pleased to hear of her success, and to see the bright intelligent faces of some native girls whom she and her companions were training. Whatever views we may entertain of the religious principles of those earnest and laborious nuns, we cannot fail to admire that courage, that Christian enthusiasm, shall I call it? which leads them to renounce the joys and luxuries of home and country, and to spend their lives amid privations, and not unfrequently dangers, in teaching these daughters of Jerusalem.

"Most of the city is very solitary and silent; echo answers to your tread; frequent waste places, among which the wild dog prowls, convey an indescribable impression of desolation. And it is not only those waste places that give such an air of loneliness to the city, but many of the streets themselves—dark, dull, and mournful-looking—seem as if the Templar's armed tread were the last to which they had resounded."

Another thing strikes the thoughtful pilgrim-traveler—the remains of the ancient city that meet the eye are singularly few: here and there a column built into a rickety wall, or a fragment of white marble in the street, or it may be a Gothic arch projecting out of a rubbish heap,— these are all that whisper memories

PORTA JUDICIARIA.

of the past. The Jerusalem of Solomon, the Jerusalem of Herod, and even to a great extent the Jerusalem of the Crusades, lies deeply buried beneath modern lanes and houses.

Another phase of the picture—strange, fantastic, incongruous—often meets the eye in street or market. A Jew, with pale, solemn visage, tattered fur-lined robe, and bearskin cap, stealing timidly along the path. Another, with heavy black turban, black girdle, and flowing Oriental gabardine, his hands folded, and his face the picture of suffering and sorrow. Behind them, perhaps, a stately Arab matron or maiden, with the light tread and free, fearless glance of her native desert, decked in holiday attire, adorned with a profusion of gold and silver ornaments and charms, the cherished collection probably

JEWS OF JERUSALEM.

This page is adjacent to a plate and is intentionally left blank.

of a long line of Bedawy matrons, and now worn to distinguish the sheikh's wife or daughter as she comes to the city on some visit of ceremony. Around her, it may be, are the brothers of her tribe, with sword and pistol, spear and match-lock, gazing round them on all passers with keen, defiant looks.

Another phase of Jerusalem life one occasionally meets with. I have encountered it more frequently, however, in Damascus and Cairo. Passing along the street, the sound of music—or at least what Orientals call music— is heard from an open *café*. Entering, we see a man, generally in the costume of a desert Arab, with flowing kerchief over his head, bound by a double fillet of camel's hair, squatting on the ground, and playing with a rude bow on an instrument which, in simplicity of design and rudeness of workmanship, might be the counterpart of that which David played before Saul. The notes are somewhat metallic, but not altogether unpleasant, and they are generally accompanied by a slow nasal

MUSICIAN IN CAFÉ.

chant one might mistake for a funeral dirge. Yet the natives of all classes enjoy it, and listen with rapt attention, as if it were the perfection of harmony and the master-piece of a musical genius.

THE CHURCH OF THE HOLY SEPULCHRE.

COULD we guarantee the genuineness of the site and the reality of the tomb, no spot in Jerusalem would be more deeply interesting than the Church of the Holy Sepulchre. This is not the place for discussing the subject, or for attempting to unravel the tangled mass of controversy regarding it. The argument for the identity of the tomb with that in which the body of our Lord was laid turns mainly on the solution of two questions—one topographical, the other historical. Jesus was crucified "without the gate," "nigh to the city," at "a place called Golgotha." The sepulchre in which he was laid was "hewn out of the rock," in a garden at the place of crucifixion. This is all we know about the site. Now the Church of the Sepulchre is far within the city; and the ancient city was unquestionably much larger than the present. Thus the topographical argument appears to be decidedly against the genuineness of the sepulchre.

The historical argument in favour of it, to say the least, is not convincing. It is not, in fact,

CHURCH OF THE HOLY SEPULCHRE.

until the fourth century—that is, until about three hundred years after the crucifixion—that we find any reference in history to the site; and during the interval the city had been repeatedly destroyed in war. Those who wish to study a subject of considerable antiquarian interest will find a *résumé* of the entire arguments, with full historical and topographical references, in my "Handbook for Syria and Palestine" (Murray's).

In this place my object is to point out and describe those holy places in the church which now attract the attention of pilgrims and travellers. I leave each to form his own opinion. The engraving shows the old tower and dome previous to recent repairs.

FELLAHAH IN HOLIDAY ATTIRE.

See page 68.

This page is adjacent to a plate and is intentionally left blank.

The Church of the Holy Sepulchre has been for fifteen hundred years the chief point of attraction to Christian pilgrims. Its history may be told in a sentence or two. Founded by the Emperor Constantine, it was dedicated in A.D. 335; Eusebius, the father of ecclesiastical history, taking part in the consecration service. It was destroyed by the Persians in 614, and rebuilt sixteen years afterwards on a new plan. It was again destroyed by the mad Khalif Hâkim, the founder of the Druse sect, and rebuilt in 1048. During the Crusades many changes and additions were made. The rotunda, the Greek church on its eastern side, the western façade,

CHURCH OF THE HOLY SEPULCHRE.
Showing Court in Front of Building as it now exists.

including the present door and tower (see Frontispiece), and the chapel over Calvary, were then erected in whole or in part. The buildings remained as the Crusaders left them till the year 1808, when they were partly destroyed by fire. They were restored, and the church, as it now stands, was consecrated in 1810.

Turning from the Via Dolorosa into a narrow lane, we soon reach an open court, its pavement worn by the feet of innumerable pilgrims, and usually littered with the wares of trinket merchants, dealers in beads, crosses, "holy" soap, and "blessed" candles, which are eagerly bought by strangers. On the northern side of the court stands the church. Its southern façade, the only one now uncovered, is a pointed Romanesque composition, dark, heavy, and yet picturesque. It has a wide double door, with detached shafts supporting richly-sculptured architraves, representing our Lord's triumphant entry into

Jerusalem. Over the door are two corresponding windows; and on the left stands the remnant of the massive campanile, once a noble tower of five stories, but now cut down to three.

On entering, it was with shame and sorrow I observed a guard of soldiers—Mohammedan soldiers—stationed in the vestibule, to keep rival Christian sects from quarrelling over the tomb of their Saviour. The principal part of the building is the *Rotunda*, which has a dome open at the top, like the Pantheon. Beneath the dome stands the *Holy Sepulchre*, a little structure, like a church in miniature, incased in white stone profusely ornamented, and surmounted by a crown-shaped cupola. It contains two small chambers—the first called the "Chapel of the Angel," and said to be the place where the angel sat after he had rolled away the stone from the door of the sepulchre. The stone itself is there too! Through this we pass, and enter the *Sepulchre* by a very low door. It is a vault, measuring six feet by seven. The tomb—a raised couch covered with a slab of white marble—occupies the whole of the right side. Over it hang forty lamps of gold and silver, kept constantly burning. I lingered long here—solemnized, almost awe-stricken—looking at pilgrim after pilgrim, in endless succession, crawling in on bended knees, putting lips and forehead and cheeks to the cold marble, bathing it with tears, then dragging himself away backwards, still in the attitude of devotion, until the threshold was again crossed. The vault *is said* to be hewn out of the rock, but not a vestige of

INTERIOR OF THE CHURCH OF THE HOLY SEPULCHRE.
Showing the Chapel of the Sepulchre.

floor, tomb, walls, are all marble. The rock *may* be there; but if so, how one should wish

> "The lichen now were free to twine
> O'er the dark entrance of that rock-hewn cell.
> Say, should we miss the gold-encrusted shrine
> Or incense-fume's intoxicating spell?"

The rotunda and sepulchre are common property. All sects—Latin, Greek, Armenian, Coptic, Jacobite—have free access to them, but each has its own establishment elsewhere. Round the Holy Sepulchre are numerous other "holy places," no less than *thirty-two* being

CHAPEL OF CALVARY, OR GOLGOTHA.

clustered under one roof! Golgotha, with its gorgeously-decorated chapel, the Stone of Unction, the Place of Apparition, the Chapel of Mocking, the Chapel of the Invention of the Cross— But why go over such a catalogue? I would not willingly mingle one light feeling or one light expression with the solemn events of the Crucifixion. Yet it is difficult to speak of these "holy places" gravely. It is difficult to forget how seriously such superstitions and traditions hinder the success of gospel truth, and how often they make Christianity a mockery in the land which gave it birth.

On another occasion, I was in the Church of the Sepulchre at Easter, when crowded with pilgrims from all lands, of all sects. It was a strange and impressive, but painful scene. In that vast crowd, with the exception of a few solitary cases, I saw nothing like devotion; and in these few cases devotional feeling had manifestly degenerated into superstition. *Place* was the object of worship, and not *God*. The bitter animosities of rival sects came out on all sides, among the clergy as well as their flocks; and it was only the presence of the Turkish guard that prevented open war. I was then glad to think that the real place of our Lord's Passion was not dishonoured. True, Christianity is a spiritual faith; it recognizes no "holy places." Yet one's natural feelings revolt at the bare idea of Calvary becoming the scene and the cause of superstition and strife.

But some of my readers will doubtless ask, "Does not the Church of the Sepulchre cover the *real* tomb of our Lord?" The question involves, as I have said, a long and tangled controversy, on which I care not to enter. I may, however, give my own first impressions on the subject—impressions which thought and study have since deepened into conviction. Before visiting Jerusalem, I knew from Scripture that Christ was crucified "without the gate." On visiting Jerusalem, I was not a little surprised to observe the dome of the Church of the Sepulchre far *within* the walls—in fact, *nearly in the centre of the city*. Yet the city in our Lord's day must have been four or five times larger than it is now. It seemed to me that topography alone makes identity impossible. But whatever may be thought of traditional "holy places," Zion and Moriah, Hinnom, Olivet, and the Kidron are there. What though the royal Palace has become "heaps," and the Temple has "not one stone left upon another"! What though the "Holy City" is "trodden down of the Gentiles," and mockery is enshrined in its sanctuary! The glens which echoed back the monarch minstrel's song, the sacred court within whose colossal walls Israel assembled to worship a present God, the hills over which Jesus walked and on whose sides he taught and prayed, the vines, the figs, the olives which suggested his beautiful parables,—all are there; and no controversies or scandals can ever change their features, or rob us of the hallowed memories they recall and the illustrations of divine truth they afford.

THE TOMBS OF JERUSALEM.

>"But we must wander witheringly
>In other lands to die;
>And where our fathers' ashes be,
>Our own may never lie."

SO may the poor Jew now sadly sing as he wanders, a despised and persecuted outcast, among the desolations of the once proud capital of his ancestors. Wherever he turns his eyes—on Zion, Moriah, Olivet—he is reminded by rock-hewn monument and yawning cave that Jerusalem is not only his holy city, but that the ashes of his ancestors are there; that it is, as the captive said in Babylon, "the place of my fathers' sepulchres."* The tombs are among the most interesting monuments of Jerusalem. The Temple "hath not left one stone;" the palaces of Solomon and Herod have long since crumbled to dust; the Jerusalem of the prophets and apostles "became heaps" centuries ago; but the tombs remain almost as perfect as when the princes of Israel were there laid "in glory, every one in his own house."† I was sadly disappointed when, after days and weeks of careful and toilsome research, I could only discover a very few authentic vestiges of "the city of the Great King;" —a few fragments of the colossal wall that inclosed the Temple courts; a few broken shafts here and there in the lanes, or protruding from some noisome rubbish heap; a few remnants of the for- tifications that once defended Zion. The most interesting of them is the Tower of Hippicus, built by Herod the Great for the defence of the northern wall and gate of Zion. The view here given is from a photograph. The Tower of David is near it. All besides is gone; buried deep, deep beneath mod- ern dwellings.

TOWER OF HIPPICUS ON ZION.

When excavat- ing for the founda- tion of the English church, portions of the old houses and aqueducts of Zion were found nearly forty feet beneath the present surface! We need not wonder that the identifica- tion of the particular buildings of primi- tive ages is now so difficult; and that even the position of the valleys which once divided the quarters of the city has become a subject of keen controversy among antiquarians. The city of Herod was built on the ruins of the city of Solomon; the city of the Crusaders was built on the ruins of the city of Herod; and modern Jerusalem is founded on the ruins of them all. Hills and cliffs have been rounded off; ravines have been filled up; palaces and fortresses have been overthrown, and their very ruins have been covered over with the rubbish of millenniums. Could David revisit

*Neh. ii. 3. †Isa. xiv. 18

his royal capital, or could Herod come back to the scene of his magnificence and his crimes, or could Godfrey rise from his tomb, so complete has been the desolation, so great the change even in the features of the site, that I believe they would find as much difficulty in settling topographical details as modern scholars do.

Nothing but excavation can settle satisfactorily and finally the vexed questions of Jerusalem's topography. A week's work in trenches would do more to solve existing mysteries than scores of volumes and years of learned research. It may well excite the wonder of Biblical scholars, that while the mounds of Assyria, Babylonia, and Chaldea have been excavated at enormous cost, so very little has been expended upon the Holy City. By judicious excavation, under the direction of accomplished antiquarians and engineers, the lines of the ancient walls, the sites of the great buildings, the sepulchres of the kings, and the beds of the valleys might all be traced. A flood of light would thus be shed upon one of the most interesting departments of Biblical topography; and who can tell what precious treasures of ancient art might still be discovered? The Palestine Exploration Fund has done much to elucidate the antiquities and topography of the Holy City; but it has been crippled by inadequate support from home, by the fanaticism of the Muslims, and by the restrictions of the Turkish Government. Will no man of influence and wealth in our country continue this work? Will no learned society contribute of its funds to carry it out? Will not our beloved Prince, who has already rendered such signal service at Hebron, render a still greater service to Biblical knowledge by encouraging such an enterprise?

It is pleasant to think that amid ruin and confusion there are still some monuments left in and around the Holy City as connecting links between the present and the distant past. The sepulchres of the Jewish nobles remain though their palaces are gone. We can see where they were buried, if we cannot see where they lived. I cannot describe with what intense emotion I heard my friends speak familiarly of the tombs of David and Absalom, of the judges, the kings, and the prophets; and what was the excited state of my feelings when they proposed one bright morning a walk to Tophet and Aceldama. Some of these places may be, and doubtless are, apocryphal; none of them may be able to stand the test of full historic investigation; but the high antiquity of the monuments themselves cannot be denied, and an inspection of them is alike interesting and instructive, from the light they throw upon the customs of God's ancient people, and from the illustrations they afford of many passages in God's Word.

Jewish Tombs.—The earliest burial-places on record were caves. When Sarah died, Abraham bought the cave of Machpelah, and buried her there. Samuel is said to have been buried "in *his house* at Ramah,"* by which, I believe, is meant *the tomb* he had

*1 Sam. xxv. i.

excavated for himself there; for the Hebrew word *beth*, "house," is sometimes used to signify a tomb, as in Isaiah xiv. 18, and Ecclesiastes xii. 5, "Man goeth to his *long home*," literally "to his *eternal house*." We read, moreover, of King Asa, that "they buried him in his own sepulchre *which he had digged for himself* in the city of David."* Elisha was buried in a *cave*;† the sepulchre of Lazarus was a *cave*;‡ and the Holy Sepulchre was a *new cave* which Joseph of Arimathea had "hewn out in the rock" for himself.§

In our own land we are all familiar with the grassy mounds and marble monuments which fill the cemeteries, and which pass away almost as quickly as man himself. In Rome and Pompeii we see the habitations of the dead lining the great highways, and crumbling to ruin like the palaces of their tenants. But the moment we set our feet on the shores of Palestine, we feel that we are in an ancient country—the home of a primeval people, whose tombs appear in cliff and glen and mountain-side, all hewn in the living rock, and permanent as the rock itself. The tombs of Jerusalem are rock-hewn caves. I found them in every direction. Wherever the face of a crag affords space for an architectural façade, or a projecting rock a fitting place for excavation, there is sure to be a sepulchre. I visited them on Olivet and Scopus, on Zion and Moriah, inside the modern city and outside; but they chiefly abound in the rocky banks of Hinnom and the Kidron. Near the junction of these ravines the overhanging cliffs are actually honeycombed. Hundreds of dark openings were in view when I stood beside En-Rogel. Some of these tombs are small grottoes, with only one or two receptacles for bodies; others are of great extent, containing chambers, galleries, passages, and *loculi*, almost without number, each tomb forming a little necropolis. The doors are low and narrow, so as to be shut by a single slab. This slab was called *golal*, that is, "a thing rolled," from the fact that it was rolled back from the opening in a groove made for it. The stone being heavy, and the groove generally inclining upwards, the operation of opening required a considerable exertion of strength. Hence the anxious inquiry of the two Marys, "Who shall *roll* us away the stone from the door of the sepulchre?"§§ The stone always fitted closely, and could easily be sealed with one of those large signets such as were then in use. Or perhaps the Holy Sepulchre may have had a wedge, or small bar, pushed into the rock behind it, like that in the tombs of the kings (described below), and preventing the stone from being rolled back. To this the seal might be attached.¶ I had always to stoop low on entering the doors, which reminded me of Peter at the sepulchre.** The façades of many are elaborately ornamented; but one thing is very remarkable, they contain no inscriptions. The tombs of Egypt are covered with hieroglyphics, giving long histories of the dead, and of the honours paid to their remains. The tombs of Palmyra not only have written tablets over the entrances, but every separate niche, or *loculus*, in the interior has

---

*2 Chron. xvi. 14. †2 Kings xiii. 21. ‡John xi. 38. §Matt. xxvii. 60. §§Mark xvi. 3. ¶Matt. xxvii. 66. **Luke xxiv. 12.

its inscription. I have counted more than fifty such in a single mausoleum; yet I have never been able to discover a single letter in one of the tombs of the Holy City, nor a single painting, sculpture, or carving on any *ancient* Jewish tomb in Palestine, calculated to throw light on the story, name, or rank of the dead.

Simplicity and security appear to have been the only things the Jews aimed at in the construction of their sepulchres. To be buried with their fathers was their only ambition. They seem to have had no desire to transmit their names to posterity through the agency of their graves. It has been well said that the words, "Let me bury my dead out of my sight"—"No man knoweth of his sepulchre unto this day," express, if not the general feeling of the Jewish nation, at least the general spirit of the Old Testament. With the Jews the tomb was an unclean place, which men endeavoured to avoid rather than honour by pilgrimages. The homage paid to them is of late date, and the offspring of a corrupt age. When near relatives died, it was, as it still is, customary for females to go and weep at their graves, as Martha and Mary did at the grave of Lazarus; but the dead were soon forgotten, and except in the case of a few of the patriarchs, kings,* and prophets,† we have no record of tombs having been even held in remembrance.

There were always a few in every age who coveted outward show and splendour in their tombs, as well as in their houses. Such was the upstart Shebna, whose vanity and pretension the prophet Isaiah describes and denounces: "What hast thou here? and whom hast thou here, that thou hast hewed thee out a sepulchre here, as he that heweth him out a sepulchre on high, that graveth an habitation for himself in a rock?"‡ It is evident that the greater part of the ornamented façades and architectural tombs are of a late date, and not purely Jewish.

Jewish Mode of Burial.—The Jews used no coffins or sarcophagi. The body was washed,§ anointed,§§ wrapped in linen cloths,¶ and laid in the niche prepared for it—an excavation about two feet wide, three high, and six deep, opening endwise in the side of the rock-chamber. The mouth of the *loculus* was then shut by a slab of stone, and sealed with cement. In some cases the bodies were laid on a kind of open shelf, such as I have seen in many of the chambers. It was thus our Lord was laid, for John tells us that Mary stooped down into the sepulchre, and seeth two angels, *the one at the head and the other at the feet*, where the body of Jesus had lain."**

The kings of Israel were buried with more pomp. In addition to the anointing of the sweet spices, "burnings" were made for them. Thus Jeremiah says to Zedekiah: "Thou shalt die in peace; and with the *burnings of thy fathers*, the former kings which were before thee, so shall they *burn* for thee." And in the case of Asa we are told there

---

*Acts vii. 16, ii. 29. †Matt. xxiii. 29. ‡Isa. xxii. 16. §Acts ix. 37. §§Mark xvi. 1; John xix. 40.
¶John xix. 40; xi. 44. **John xx. 11, 12.

was "a great burning."* It is not meant that the bodies were burned, but that sweet spices and perfumes were burned in honour of the dead, and probably in their sepulchres. The bodies of Saul and Jonathan are the only ones which we read of as having been burned.†

The Tomb of David.—On the southern brow of Zion, outside the modern walls, there is a little group of buildings distinguished from afar by a dome and minaret. These, according to an old tradition, believed in alike by Jews, Christians, and Mohammedans, cover the sepulchre of Israel's minstrel king. As matters now stand, the truth of the tradition can neither be proved nor disproved. The Turks esteem the spot one of their very holiest shrines, and they will neither examine it themselves nor permit others to do so. No place about Jerusalem, not even the

THE CŒNACULUM AND TOMB OF DAVID.

Haram, is guarded with such jealousy. I visited the building frequently; I walked round and through it; I peeped into every hole, window, and passage accessible to me; I tried soft words and even a liberal *bakshish* with the gentlemanly old keeper: but it was all in vain; I saw no more than my predecessors had done.

The principal apartment in the group of buildings is a Gothic chamber, evidently a Christian church of the Crusading age, though probably built on an older site, or perhaps reconstructed out of an earlier model. Tradition has filled it with "holy places," making it the scene of the Last Supper (hence its name *Cœnaculum*), of the meeting of the disciples after the resurrection, of the miracle of Pentecost, of the residence and death of

*2 Chron. xvi. 14. †1 Sam. xxxi. 11-13.

the Virgin, and of the burial of Stephen. At its eastern end is a little chancel where Romish priests sometimes celebrate mass; and on the south side is a *mihrab* where Muslems pray. It is thus a centre of tradition, superstition, and imposture.

The crypt is the real holy place. A portion of it has been walled off and consecrated as a mosque-mausoleum. So sacred is it, that none have the *entrée*—not even Muslem santons or grandees—except the sheikh who keeps it, and the members of his family. Fürer, a German traveller of the sixteenth century, tells us he gained access to it; and he probably saw the interior. In 1839 Sir Moses Montefiore was permitted to approach an iron railing and look into the chamber which contains the tomb; but he could not enter. The Jew is shut out alike from the temple and tombs of his fathers.

Miss Barclay, a young American lady (daughter of the author of "The City of the Great King"), has been more fortunate. She gained admission to the mausoleum with a female friend, a near relative of the keeper; she spent an hour in the sanctuary, took a sketch of the interior, and has given us the following description of what she saw:—"The room is insignificant in its dimensions, but is furnished very gorgeously. The tomb is apparently an immense sarcophagus of rough stone, and is covered by green satin tapestry, richly embroidered with gold. A satin canopy, of red, blue, green, and yellow stripes, hangs over the tomb; and another piece of black velvet tapestry, embroidered in silver, *covers a door in one end of the room which, they said, leads to a cave underneath*. Two tall silver candlesticks stand before this door, and a little lamp hangs in a window near it, which is kept constantly burning...The ceiling of the room is vaulted, and the walls covered with blue porcelain in floral figures."

Such then is the present state of the reputed Tomb of David. It is well known, however, that the Muslems carefully shut up their most sacred shrines, and construct others either directly over them or close beside them, which they visit and venerate as the real places. So it is at the Tomb of Abraham in Hebron, and so, doubtless, it is here. The real sepulchre, if here at all, is in a vault beneath, and the door mentioned by Miss Barclay probably leads to it. No fact in the Bible is more plainly stated than this, that David, and most of his successors on the throne of Israel, were buried in the "city of David;" that is, in Zion.* The royal sepulchres were well known after the return of the Jews from Babylon, and Nehemiah incidentally describes their position.† Josephus says that Solomon buried David with great pomp, and placed immense treasures in his tomb. These remained undisturbed until Hyrcanus, when besieged by Antiochus, opened one room and took out three thousand talents to buy off the enemy. Herod the Great also plundered the tomb; and it is said that two of his guards were killed by a flame that burst upon them when engaged in the sacrilegious act. We have a still later testimony to the preservation of the tomb in the words of the apostle Peter regarding David:—

---

*1 Kings ii. 10; xi. 43; xv. 24, etc.   †Neh. iii. 15, 16

"His sepulchre is with us unto this day."* We hear no more of it till the twelfth century, when Benjamin of Tudela relates the following strange story, which I insert as perhaps having some slight foundation in fact:—

"On Mount Zion are the sepulchres of the house of David. In consequence of the following circumstance, this place is hardly to be recognized. Fifteen years ago one of the walls of the church on Zion fell down, and the Patriarch ordered the priest to repair it, and to take the stones requisite from the old wall of Zion....Two labourers, when thus employed, found a stone which covered the mouth of a cave. This they entered in search of treasures, and reached a large hall, supported by pillars of marble, encrusted with gold and silver, and before which stood a table with a golden sceptre and crown. This was the sepulchre of David; to the left they saw that of Solomon in a similar state; and so on the sepulchres of the other kings buried there. They saw chests locked up, and were on the point of entering when a blast of wind rushing out threw them lifeless on the ground. They lay there senseless until evening, and then they heard a voice commanding them to go forth from the place. The Patriarch on hearing the story ordered the tomb to be walled up." The royal sepulchres were doubtless hewn in the rock, like all those of great men in that age; and they must still exist. Excavation, or at least a full exploration of the place, will alone solve the mystery. Of one thing we may be assured, that the sepulchre of David cannot have been far distant from the building now said to stand over it.

Tophet.—On one occasion, after a long visit to Zion, I walked down through the terraced corn-fields on its southern declivity into the deep glen of Hinnom. The sun was low in the west, and the ravine, with its rugged cliffs, and dusky olive groves, was thrown into deep shadow. Not a human being was there, and no sound from the city broke in upon the silence. The high rocks along the whole southern bank are honeycombed with tombs, whose dark mouths made the place look still more gloomy. Already the jackals had left their lairs, and numbers of them ran out and in of the sepulchres, and were prowling among the rocks and through the olive trees. As I wandered on down Hinnom towards the Kidron, I observed that the tombs became more and more numerous, until at length, at the junction of the valleys, every available spot in the surrounding cliffs and rocks was excavated. They are mostly plain chambers, or groups of chambers opening into one another, hewn in the soft limestone, without any attempt at ornament, save, here and there, a moulding round the door. I observed a few Hebrew and Greek inscriptions, but of late date—certainly not older than the ninth or tenth century.

Here, in the mouth of Hinnom, was situated the *Tophet* of the Bible,—originally,

*Acts ii. 29

perhaps, a "music bower," or "pleasure garden" of Solomon's; but afterwards desecrated by lust, and defiled by the offerings of Baal and the fires of

> "Moloch, horrid king, besmeared with blood
> Of human sacrifice and parents' tears."

It finally became so notorious for its abominations that it was regarded as the "very type of hell;" and the name of the valley, Ge-Hinnom, in Greek *Gehenna*, was given by the Jews to the infernal regions. Jeremiah gives some terrible sketches of the atrocities perpetrated on this spot in the name of religion;* he depicts the judgments which the Lord pronounced on the city and people on account of them.† Standing in the bed of the valley I saw how literally one part of the curse had been fulfilled: "Wherefore the days come when it shall no more be called Tophet, nor the valley of Ben-Hinnom, but the valley of Slaughter; *for they shall bury in Tophet till there be no place.*"‡ And as I returned that evening up the Kidron to my home on Olivet, I saw what seemed to me another terrible illustration of the outpouring of the curse. I saw hyenas, jackals, and vultures tearing the corpses from the shallow graves in the modern Jewish cemetery. With what harrowing vividness did the prophet's dire prediction then flash upon my mind: "*Their carcases will I give to be meat for the fowls of heaven, and for the beasts of the earth.* And I will make this city desolate, and an hissing; every one that passeth thereby shall be astonished and hiss, because of all the plagues thereof!"§

Aceldama.—On another occasion I went to the necropolis of Tophet for a double purpose,—to explore the rock tombs more thoroughly, and to see the painting of the Valley of Jehoshaphat, which the lamented Mr. Seddon was just then completing. He had pitched his little tent at the door of an old sepulchre on the brow of the hill; and as we approached an armed goat-herd was before him, whom he was working into the foreground. I was equally delighted and surprised, as I have already said, at the faithfulness of colouring and the accuracy of detail in that admirable picture. He kindly left his work, and walked away with us to Aceldama. Another artist was of our party, who was then reproducing, with all the vividness and faithfulness of reality, the scene of THE FINDING OF CHRIST IN THE TEMPLE. That day will remain one of the sunny spots on memory's clouded landscape.

Tomb after tomb we passed and explored, lighting up their gloomy chambers and narrow *loculi* with our torches, and wondering at the endless variety and numbers of these homes of the forgotten dead. At length we reached a narrow ledge or terrace, on the steep bank, directly facing the Pool of Siloam. Here was a large square edifice, half excavated in the living rock, half built of massive masonry. Looking in through a rent

---

*Jer. vii. 31.   †Jer. xix. 6-15.   ‡Jer. vii. 32.   §Jer. xix. 7, 8.

in the wall, we found that it was a vast charnel-house, some twenty feet deep, the bottom covered with dust and mouldering bones. This is ACELDAMA, "the field of blood," bought with the "thirty pieces of silver, the price of Him that was valued, whom they of the children of Israel did value."* The tradition which identifies it is at least as old as the fourth century; and it is a remarkable fact that the peculiar clay on the adjoining terraces would seem to show that this had once been a "potter's field." "They took counsel, and bought with them the *potter's field*, to bury strangers in."†

Siloam.—I had been often struck with the quaint and picturesque appearance of the little hamlet of *Silwân*, whose houses seem to cling like swallows' nests to the gray cliffs of Olivet. It

VILLAGE OF SILOAM.

takes its name from the fountain on the opposite side of the Kidron, at the base of Moriah; and it alone brings down to modern times the sacred name of "the waters of *Shiloah* that flow softly,"‡ and of that "pool of *Siloam*" in which our Lord commanded the blind man to wash.§ Its inhabitants have a bad name, and are known to be lawless, fanatical vagabonds. I resolved, however, to explore their den; and I succeeded, notwithstanding repeated threats and curses, intermixed now and again with a stone or two. I was well repaid. The village stands on a necropolis; and the habitations are half caves, half buildings,—a single room, or rude porch, being attached to the front of a rock tomb. It is a strange, wild place. On every side I heard children's prattle issuing from the gloomy chambers of ancient sepulchres. Looking into one, I saw an infant cradled in an old sarcophagus. The larger tombs, where the ashes of Israel's nobles once

*Matt. xxvii. 9.   †Matt. xxvii. 7.   ‡Isa. viii. 6.   §John ix. 7.

reposed, were now filled with sheep and goats, and lambs and kids gambolled merrily among the *loculi*. The steep hill-side appears to have been hewn into irregular terraces, and along these the sepulchres were excavated, one above another. They are better finished than those of Tophet; and a few of them are Egyptian in style, and may, perhaps, be of that age when Egyptian influence was strong at the court of Solomon.*

There is one tomb at the north end of the village, shown on the left of the engraving, deserving of special note. It is a monolith, hewn out of the side of the hill. It resembles in form

ABSALOM'S TOMB.

some of the tombs of Egypt; and a well-known but rather enthusiastic French traveller affirms that it is the chapel where Solomon's Egyptian wife performed the sacred rites of her native country, not being permitted to do so within the city or Temple courts.

Absalom's Pillar.—The most picturesque group of sepulchral monuments around the Holy City is that in the valley of the Kidron, just beneath the south-east angle of the Haram.

*1 Kings vii. 8-12; xi. 8;   2 Chron. viii. 11.

There are four tombs here in a range (see engraving, page 28), which from their position in the deep narrow glen, and from the style of their architecture, cannot fail to arrest the attention of every visitor to the Holy City. I walked up to them from Siloam. That was a sad walk. I can never forget the horrid sights I saw. The whole side of Olivet is covered with Jewish graves. In most cases the bodies have only a few inches of loose earth thrown over them, and then a broad stone is laid on the top. All round me were revolting evidences of the carnival held nightly there by dogs, jackals, and hyenas. Vultures were enjoying a horrid banquet within a stone's-throw of me; and gorged with food, they seemed fearless of my approach. Never before had the degradation to which the poor Jews must now submit been brought before my mind with such harrowing vividness.

> "Tribes of the wandering foot and weary breast,
> How shall you flee away and be at rest?
> The wild-dove hath her nest, the fox his cave,
> Mankind their country,—Israel but the grave!"

The *Tomb* or *Pillar of Absalom* is a cubical structure, the lower part hewn out of the rock, measuring twenty-two feet on each side, and ornamented with Ionic pilasters. It is surmounted by a circular cone of masonry, terminating in a tuft of palm leaves. In the interior is a small excavated chamber, with two niches for bodies. The architecture shows at once that this cannot be the "pillar" which Absalom had "reared up for himself during his lifetime in the king's dale;"* and, indeed, his name was only attached to it about the twelfth century. It resembles some of the tombs of Petra, and may, perhaps, be the work of one of the Herods, who were of Idumean descent.

A few yards south is another monolithic structure, somewhat resembling the preceding, and now usually called the *Tomb of Zacharias*—that Zacharias who was stoned in the court of the Temple in the reign of Joash,† and to whom Christ refers as slain between the Temple and the altar.‡ But there is no evidence to connect the monument with this or any other Old Testament worthy. The Jews hold it in high veneration; and the dearest wish of their hearts is to have their bones laid beside it. The whole ground around it is crowded with graves.

Between these two monuments is a large chamber excavated in the side of the cliff, having a Doric porch supported by two columns. Within it are several vaults, and numerous *loculi* for bodies. Here, says tradition, the Apostle James found an asylum during the interval between the crucifixion and the resurrection. The story is, of course, apocryphal, and was not attached to the tomb till about the fourteenth century. The view of the Kidron valley from this spot is singularly impressive. There is nothing like it in Palestine, or elsewhere. The valley is deep, rugged, and altogether destitute of

*2 Sam. xviii. 18.   †2 Chron. xxiv. 21.   ‡Matt. xxiii. 35.

verdure. On one side Moriah rises in banks of naked rock and bare shelving acclivities, until it is crowned, far overhead, by the colossal wall of the Haram; on the other side the limestone cliffs are hewn out into architectural façades, and monuments, and yawning sepulchre; while away above them, here and there, a patriarchal olive, with sparse branches and great gnarled arms, stands forsaken and desolate, like the last tree of a forest.

The Tombs of the Prophets.—High up on the brow of Olivet, between the footpath that leads to the Church of the Ascension and the main road to Bethany, is a very remarkable catacomb, of the most ancient Jewish type. It is called *The Tombs of the Prophets*, though there is no inscription, or historical memorial, or even ancient tradition, to justify the name. Equipped in a "working costume," and furnished with a handful of little candles, we started early one morning to explore it. Crawling into a narrow hole in an open field, and then down a long gallery, we reached a circular vault, twenty-four feet in diameter; from it two parallel galleries, five feet wide and ten feet high, are carried through the rock for some twenty yards; a third runs in another direction; and they are all connected by cross galleries, the outer one of which is forty yards in length, and has a range of thirty *loculi* for bodies. The

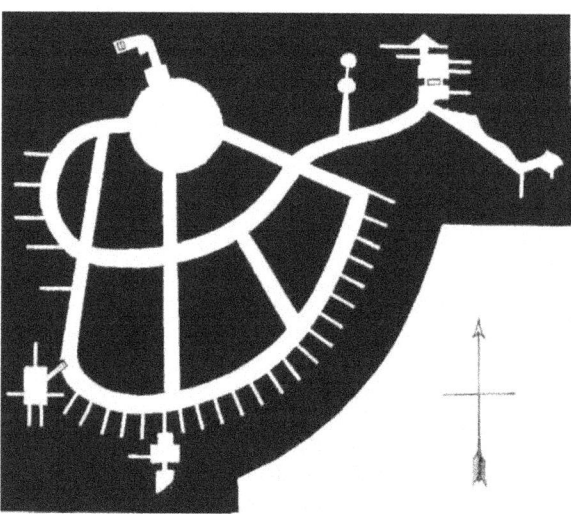

PLAN OF THE TOMB OF THE PROPHETS.

accompanying diagram will show the intricate plan and singular structure of these interesting tombs better than any description.

Church and Tomb of the Virgin.—On coming forth again to the light of day, which, after the darkness, seemed doubly brilliant, we descended the hill-side, and paid a passing visit to the tomb of Mary. It is a quaint but singularly picturesque structure, and must excite the admiration of every pilgrim to Gethsemane and Olivet. Gray and worn with age, deeply set among the rocky roots of the mount, shaded by venerable olive trees, it is one of those buildings which even all the absurdity of tradition cannot divest of interest. On entering the door we had a long descent by some sixty steps to the chapel, a gloomy, rugged, natural cave, partly remodelled by human hands. Here tradition has placed the empty tomb of the Virgin, and has located the scene of the Assumption.

We walked on up the glen, through olive groves which seem denser and more ancient than anywhere else round the city. The rocky banks on both sides, but especially on that next Jerusalem, are filled with tombs; and I felt strongly impressed that some one of these was that "new tomb" which Joseph of Arimathea "had hewn for himself" in his garden, and in which Jesus was laid. Continuing our walk, we saw traces of Agrippa's wall on the brow of the glen. Then, after crossing the Anathoth road, and turning westward, we came upon more sepulchres, with richly-ornamented doorways. But by far the most magnificent sepulchre in this region, and indeed around Jerusalem, is the so-called

Tomb of the Kings.—This remarkable catacomb is half a mile from the city, not far from the great northern road. On reaching the spot we find a broad trench, hewn in the rock to the

CHURCH AND TOMB OF THE VIRGIN.

depth of eighteen feet. An inclined plane leads down to it. Then we pass, by a very low doorway, through a wall of rock seven feet thick, into a court ninety-two feet long, eighty-seven broad, and about twenty deep, all excavated in the rock. The sides are hewn smooth. On the western side is a vestibule, originally supported by two columns. The front has a deep frieze and cornice, ornamented with clusters of grapes, triglyphs, and paterae, alternating over a continuous garland of fruit and foliage, which was carried down the sides. Unfortunately this beautiful façade is almost obliterated. When perfect it must have been magnificent.

The entrance to the tomb is at the southern end of the vestibule. The door, with its approaches and fastenings, is one of the most remarkable and ingenious pieces of mechanism which has come down to us from antiquity. The whole is now in a ruinous state, but enough remains to show what it once was. The door could only be reached by a subterranean passage, the entrance to which was by a small trap-door in the floor of the vestibule; and when reached, it was found to be covered by a circular stone, like a small millstone, which had to be "rolled away" to the side, up an inclined plane. In addition to this there was another large stone, which could be slid in behind the door, at right angles, along a concealed groove, and which held it immovably in its place. And there was, besides, an inner door of stone, opening on a pivot, and shutting by its own weight. The interior arrangements of this splendid monument will be best understood by the accompanying plan. In one respect it differs from all the other sepulchres yet known about Jerusalem—the inner chamber, which is several feet lower than any of the others, formerly contained two sarcophagi of white marble, beautifully ornamented with wreaths of flowers. The more perfect of them was carried away by M. de Saulcy, and placed in the museum of the Louvre. The other is in fragments.

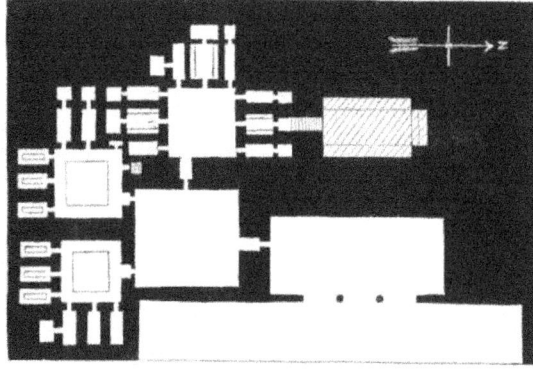

PLAN OF THE TOMB OF THE KINGS.

Even this tomb contains no record of its history. The memory and the names of those who were laid here in royal state cannot now be ascertained with certainty. There is a high probability that it was the sepulchre of Helena, the widowed queen of Adiabene. It is known that she became a proselyte to Judaism, resided in the Holy City during the apostolic age, and made for herself a great sepulchre. Able scholars have questioned the identity. Be this as it may, we have here a costly, grand, and strongly guarded sepulchre, now opened, wrecked, and rifled, as if to show that man's home is not, cannot be, on earth.

Other celebrated tombs I visited and explored: the *Tombs of the Judges*, a mile farther north; the *Tomb of El Musahny*, recently discovered, and of the earliest Jewish type; the *Tomb of Helena*, etc. I need not describe them. The general plan of all is the same; and all are equally without story, without name, and without tenant. The hand of the spoiler has not spared the ashes of fallen, outcast Israel. The tombs have all been rifled. The bones and the ashes of the mighty dead have been swept away, and desolation reigns supreme even in the sepulchres of Jerusalem. The time foretold by Jeremiah has long since come: "At that time, saith the Lord, they shall bring out the bones of the kings of Judah, and the bones of his princes, and the bones of the priests, and the bones of the inhabitants of Jerusalem, out of their graves: and they shall spread them before the sun, and the moon, and all the host of heaven….they shall not be gathered nor be buried; they shall be for dung upon the face of the earth."*

*Jer. viii. 1, 2.

THE FOUNTAIN OF THE VIRGIN AND POOL OF SILOAM.

A RECENT tradition has given the name *Fountain of the Virgin* to one of the most remarkable fountains around Jerusalem. Like many another local tradition, it probably owes its origin to the lively imagination and ready invention of Orientals. The fountain is in the valley of the Kidron, just below the village of Siloam. It rises from the bottom of a deep cave at the base of Ophel. The masonry in the sides of the cave is ancient. A long flight of steps leads down to the water, which issues from under the lowest step, flows across the bottom of the cave, and disappears, with a weird, murmuring sound, into a narrow, dark, rock-hewn tunnel.

What has given this fountain, both in ancient and modern times, its greatest celebrity is the intermittent flow of the water. It was noticed by Dr. Edward Robinson, who has written the following interesting account of his experience:—

"As we were preparing to measure the basin, and explore the passage leading from it, my companion was standing on the lower step, with one foot on a loose stone in the basin. All at once he perceived the water coming into his shoe; and supposing the stone had rolled, he withdrew his foot to the step, which, however, was also now covered with water. This excited our curiosity, and we perceived the water rapidly bubbling up from under the step. In less than five minutes it had risen in the basin nearly or quite a foot, and we could hear it gurgling off through the interior passage. In ten minutes more it had ceased to flow." A woman, who was accustomed to wash at the fountain daily, informed them that the flowing occurs at irregular intervals—sometimes two or three times a day, and sometimes only once in two or three days.

The common legend is, that a dragon lies within the fountain: when awake he stops the water, when he sleeps it flows. Instead of a dragon the Jews believed an angel was the cause.

Dr. Robinson gives a romantic account of his exploration of the tunnel in company with a fellow-traveller, Dr. Eli Smith. It was rather a dangerous adventure, and is worth recital. Having put on aquatic costume, and provided candles and matches, they entered the passage. At first they had little difficulty, as the cutting was high. Soon they were obliged to proceed on hands and knees; and then the passage became so low that they "could only get forward by lying at full length and dragging themselves along upon their elbows." Just at the lowest part they suddenly heard behind them the murmuring flow of the water. It rose to within a few inches of the rock, and they had much difficulty in finding breathing space above the stream. It was an anxious moment. For some minutes death seemed imminent. Gradually, however, to their intense relief, the murmuring ceased, the water fell, and they worked their toilsome way onward. At length light dawned in front, and they emerged through an arched opening in the end of the *Pool of Siloam*. The total length of the tunnel is about six hundred yards, but it is crooked.

The Fountain of the Virgin is most probably the "king's pool" mentioned by Nehemiah as the place where, in his night survey of the fortifications, there was no way for the beast he rode to pass. "Then," he says, " went I up in the night by the brook, and viewed the wall."* Long afterwards Josephus calls it Solomon's Reservoir. It would no doubt serve an important purpose in the history, and especially during the sieges, of Jerusalem. The tunnel was manifestly constructed to convey the water from an exposed fountain by a subterranean passage to a reservoir within the walls.

The Pool of Siloam.—No water about Jerusalem has obtained such a wide celebrity as

> "Siloa's brook, that flowed
> Fast by the oracle of God."

Yet it is only thrice mentioned in the Bible. Isaiah speaks of "the waters of Shiloah that go softly;"† Nehemiah tells us that Shallum built "the wall of the pool of Siloah by the king's garden;"‡ and then, most interesting of all, we have our Lord's command to the blind man, "Go, wash in the pool of Siloam. He went his way therefore, and washed, and came seeing."§ Josephus describes its position so clearly as to leave no doubt regarding its identity.

In going from the Fountain of the Virgin to the pool, we walk down the Kidron to an open place of corn-fields, dotted with trees, where the Tyropœon falls into it. This is the "King's Garden." Across the Tyropœon is an old embankment, on the end of which stands a venerable mulberry tree, now in the last stage of decay, and supported by a pile of stones. Here again tradition has been busy, and informs us that the tree marks the spot where Manasseh caused the prophet Isaiah to be sawn asunder: hence its name, *Isaiah's Tree*.

Turning to the right we pass the projecting cliff of Ophel, ascend the bank, and soon stand beside Siloah's Pool. It is a large reservoir, built mainly of comparatively modern masonry. In the sides, however, are some limestone shafts of a much earlier date; originally designed, probably, to support a roof. At the upper end we observe the arched passage opening into the tunnel above described, which brings the water from the Virgin's Fountain. The discovery of the connection between the fountain and the pool explains

---

*Neh. ii. 14, 15.   †Isa. viii. 6.   ‡Neh. iii. 15.   §John ix. 7.

POOL OF SILOAM.

This page is adjacent to a plate and is intentionally left blank.

the reason why Siloam has from a remote age been spoken of as an intermittent fountain. Jerome remarks that its "waters do not flow regularly, but on certain days and hours, and issue with a great noise from caverns in the rock."

May not Siloam, or the Virgin's Fountain, be that *Pool of Bethesda* into which, according to the Jewish tradition, an angel went down at a certain season and troubled the water; whosoever then first after the troubling of the water stepped in was made whole of whatsoever disease he had"?* The evangelist does not seem to vouch for the truth of the tradition; he introduces it to explain the circumstance of our Lord's healing the impotent man. The troubling of the water would be a popular explanation of the strange phenomenon of an intermittent spring, accompanied by such murmuring sound as that which I have described. There is little else, however, to identify Bethesda with Siloam.

OLIVET AND BETHANY.

"In the day-time he was teaching in the temple; and at night he went out, and abode in the mount that is called the mount of Olives."—LUKE xxi. 37.

THE name Olivet goes direct to the Christian's heart, and awakens the deepest and holiest feelings there. It recalls so many memories of Jesus,—of his wondrous power and still more wondrous love,—of his human sympathies and his divine teachings,—of the greatness of his agony and the glories of his triumph,—that the heart overflows with love and gratitude the moment the name falls upon the ear. With Gethsemane on one side and Bethany on the other; with paths, well marked, connecting them, often trodden by the Son of man; with gardens of olives and vineyards between, where he was wont to pray for his people and weep for a sinful world; with one spot upon those terraced slopes overlooking the wilderness, where his feet stood on the eve of the Ascension, and where his wondering disciples received from white-robed angels the joyous promise of his second advent;—with these hallowed associations clustering round it, surely it will be admitted that, above and beyond all places in Palestine, Olivet witnessed "GOD MANIFEST IN FLESH,"

"Here may we sit and dream
Over the heavenly theme,
Till to our soul the former days return.
*   *   *   *
Or choose thee out a cell
In Kidron's storied dell,

*John v. 4.

> Beside the springs of love that never die;
> Among the olives kneel,
> The chill night blast to feel,
> And watch the moon that saw thy Master's agony."

Yet I was disappointed in Olivet; not in its associations—no Christian could be disappointed in these—but in its appearance. One always expects to find something in a holy or historic place worthy of its history. Here there is nothing. When approaching Jerusalem from the west I looked, but I looked in vain, for any "mountain" or even "mount" that the eye could at once rest on and identify as Olivet. Beyond the gray battlements of the city lay a long *ridge*, barely overtopping the Castle of David and the higher buildings on Zion: drooping to the right, it opens a view of the distant mountains of Moab; and running away far to the north, it fills in the whole background. This is Olivet. It has no striking features. It is rounded, regular, colourless; and the air is so clear and the colouring so defective that it seems to rise immediately out of the city. In the distance the outline is almost horizontal; but as one draws near it becomes wavy, and at length three tops or eminences can be distinguished, the central and highest crowned with the dome and minaret of the "Church of the Ascension," and the other two about equi-distant to the right and left. Photographs show these peculiarities, and consequently look flat and uninteresting.

When I passed round the city and stood on the brow of the Kidron, at the north-east angle of the wall, the view was much more impressive; in fact, this is one of the most picturesque views about Jerusalem. Olivet *now* assumed the appearance of a "mount." At my feet was the deep glen, shaded with dusky olive groves; and from the bottom swelled up in gray terraced slopes and gray limestone crags, nearly six hundred feet, the hill-side. Close on my right was the city wall, running south in a straight line near—not *upon*—the rocky edge of the ravine, till it joined the loftier and more massive wall of the Haram. The depth of the Kidron and the comparative elevation and respective positions of Moriah and Olivet are seen from this point to great advantage. The sides of the two hills meet, and here and there overlap in the bottom of the narrow crooked glen; while the summits are barely half a mile apart,—Olivet overtopping its sister three hundred feet. The side of Moriah is steep and bare as if scarped; while the whole of Olivet is cultivated in little terraced fields of wheat and barley, intermixed with a few straggling vines trailing along the ground or hanging over the rude terrace walls. Fig-trees are seen at intervals, but olives are still, as they were in our Lord's days, the prevailing trees on the mount. It has as good a title now as it perhaps ever had to the name "Olivet." Olive-trees dot it all over; in some places far apart, in others closer together, though nowhere so close as to form groves. Most of them are old, gnarled, and stunted, a few are propped up and in the last stage of decay; I saw scarcely any young, vigorous trees.

I endeavoured, when residing on the Mount of Olives, to localize every incident of Scripture history of which it was the scene, to bring together the sacred narrative and the sacred place; so to group, in fact, the various actors on the spots where they acted, that the stories might be made to assume to my mind, as far as possible, the semblance of reality. I tried to follow every footstep of David, and of David's greater Son; to recall every circumstance, and note every local characteristic, and every topographical feature that might illustrate the prophecies and parables, the discourses, miracles, and walks of our Lord. Some of the leading points are fixed and cannot be mistaken, such as Bethany and Jerusalem, and the one great road from the city, deeply cut in zigzag lines down the steep side of Moriah from St. Stephen's Gate to the bridge over the Kidron. Then there are the two main roads over Olivet to Bethany, branching at the bridge: the one crossing the summit almost in a straight line, is steep, rugged, and only fit for pedestrians or active cavaliers; the other, diverging to the right, winds round the southern shoulder of the hill, and is easier and better adapted for caravans and processions. Many difficulties met me in the arrangement of details. Gradually, however, they cleared away. Daily study of the Record, and daily examination of the Mount, removed one after another, until at length the texts and places, the stories and the scenes, so completely harmonized and blended that they formed one series of graphic and vivid life-pictures.

I shall now try to show my reader what I saw myself, and make Olivet to him what it must ever henceforth be to me—one of the most venerated and instructive spots on earth. True, Christianity is not a religion of "holy places;" on the contrary, the whole spirit of the gospel, the whole writings and teachings of our Lord and his apostles, tend to withdraw men's minds from an attachment to places, and to lead them to worship a spiritual God "in spirit and in truth." It was not without a wise purpose that the exact scenes of the Annunciation, the Nativity, the Crucifixion, the Resurrection, and the Ascension were left unknown; and that these events themselves were made to stand altogether unconnected with places, giving no sanctity to them, and deriving no superior efficacy from them. God thus took away all ground and excuse for that spirit of superstition which will only offer its incense at an earthly shrine. He showed that Christianity was designed to be the religion of the world, and not merely of Palestine,—that the story of Jesus and his salvation was written not for one nation, but to be read and understood equally by all mankind.

This is true; and yet it is no less true that when we stand upon the spot where the discourses of the gospel were delivered, or where the incidents of the gospel occurred,—when we look upon the very objects which called forth the sayings of our Lord, or which gave a turn and a point to his language, or which furnished his illustrations, or which formed the subjects of his prophetic denunciations,—a flood of light is thrown upon the record, and the various statements, discourses, and stories assume a freshness, a life-like vividness, which equally delight and astonish us.

It is difficult for those who have spent all their lives in a cold, inhospitable Western clime to understand the peculiarities of the East. Orientals pass most of their days and nights in the open air. Except in the cold of winter, the house is used among the middle and lower classes more for privacy than for residence. During nine months in the year to bivouac is, as a rule, a positive luxury. Within, the houses are oppressive, the ventilation is bad, the chambers are rarely, if ever, perfectly clean; so that the terrace roof, or the garden, or the vineyard, or the

TRAVELLERS' CAMP.

open hill-side, is far more pleasant for rest and sleep. Travellers generally prefer the balmy air of their tents to the stuffy city hotel. Such has been my experience. And even now, amid the splendours of Western civilization and the luxurious trappings of an English bed-room, I have many a time longed for the freshness and untrammelled freedom of my camp and my tent—even for a bivouac amid the hills of Judah. The clear, starry nights, and early mornings, are wonderfully invigorating. Reading the stories of Jacob at Beth-el, of the Israelites in the desert, of David amid the cliffs of En-gedi, of Elijah by the brook Cherith, and of our Lord and his disciples on

Olivet, I can realize their true position, in so far at least as external privations are concerned.

Gethsemane.—It would appear that our Lord, during his visits to Jerusalem, never spent a night in the city. Sometimes he walked to Bethany, but usually he made the Mount of Olives his home. Thus we read in John, "Every man went unto his own house. *Jesus went unto the mount of Olives.*"* And Luke, narrating the events of another visit, says, "In the day-time he was teaching in the temple; and at night he went out, *and abode in the mount that is called the mount of Olives.*"† A habit is here spoken of,—the usual practice of our Lord; as is still more plainly intimated in the story of his betrayal,—"He came out, and went, *as he was wont*, to the mount of Olives."‡ It appears, moreover, that there was one particular "place" on the mount to which he was accustomed to go, and in which to stay; for it is added, "And when he was *at the place*, he said," etc. John informs us that this "place" was a garden—an enclosure planted with trees;§ and that it was "over the brook Cedron"—that is, on the other side from Jerusalem. Matthew and Mark give us the name of the "garden,"—"Then cometh Jesus with them unto *a place* called GETHSEMANE," or "oil-press;" doubtless because there was an oil-press in the garden, as there usually is connected with every olive-yard.§§

Here, then, we have a most interesting trait in the character of Jesus; and we have a spot indicated which is more closely connected than any other with his private life. After wearing and toilsome labours during the day in the crowded streets of the city, after jarring controversies with Scribes and Pharisees in the Temple courts, he was accustomed to retire in the evening with his disciples to this garden, and there spend the night in peaceful seclusion. And when fanaticism broke forth into open persecution—when an infatuated populace cried for his blood, and took up stones to stone him—passing through them, he found an asylum in the deep shade of Gethsemane.¶ Here, too, he had his *oratory*, where he was wont to pray. On the night of his betrayal, when he had led his disciples to "the garden," he said, "Sit ye here, while I go and pray *yonder*;"** no doubt indicating some well-known spot away in the deeper shade of the olive-trees. There is a strong probability, too, that this was that "*certain place*" mentioned by Luke where Jesus was praying when, at the request of his disciples, he taught them the Lord's Prayer.†† It may have been to this very place Nicodemus came by night, having heard the secret of the Saviour's retreat from some of his followers, or perhaps having been himself the owner of the garden.

That the Son of man should have his house in a garden—that he should be forced to rest, and sleep, and pray on the hill-side, under the open canopy of heaven—must seem to

---

*John vii. 53, viii. 1. †Luke xxi. 37. ‡Luke xxi. 39; see also John xviii. 2. §κηπος, John xviii. 1.
§§Matt. xxvi. 36; Mark xiv. 32. ¶John viii. 59; Luke x. 25-38. **Matt. xxvi. 36. ††Luke xi. 1, x. 38-42.

many passing strange. It looks like a practical commentary on his own touching declaration: "The foxes have holes, and the birds of the air have nests, but the Son of man hath not where to lay his head." May we not ask, however, "If there was no house in Jerusalem that would shelter, no friend there that would welcome him, was not Bethany near? Was there not a home for him in the house of Martha? Why did he not go to Bethany?" Those familiar with Eastern life will easily understand the whole matter. Nearly all the inhabitants of Palestine sleep during a great part of the year in the open air. It is common for families to leave their

GETHSEMANE AS IT IS.

houses in town or village early in the spring, and bivouac under a tree or rude arbour the whole summer. Travellers, when about to spend a few days or weeks at a town or village, generally rent a garden and live there. I have often done so myself, and have slept with the earth for a bed, and the starry sky for a canopy. There is no rain, and no dew; the ground is dry, and the fresh balmy air of the country is far preferable to the close, stifling atmosphere of an Eastern city. Another thing must not be overlooked. As society is constituted in the East, one can have no privacy in a strange house, night or day. The *one* apartment in which the males sit, sleep, and eat, is open to all comers. If we would meditate or pray, we must go, like Peter, to the house-top;* or, like Isaac, to the field;† or, like Jesus, to a mountain.‡ Our

*Acts x.9.   †Gen. xxiv. 63.   ‡Luke vi. 12.

Lord desired a place where he could be alone with his disciples, and alone with his Father; and he chose the garden on Olivet. Most probably it belonged to some secret friend, who placed it at his disposal. Be this as it may, his followers knew it well: "and Judas also, which betrayed him, knew the place; for Jesus ofttimes resorted thither with his disciples."*

Often and often I have walked from Jerusalem to the Mount of Olives: by day, in the full blaze of sunlight; at even, when the shadows were deep in the Kidron; in the still night, when the moon shed her pale silvery beams on gray crag and dusky tree. Now I wandered round the southern angle of the Haram, past those great old stones, and along the brow of the glen; now I went straight down from the city gate; now round by the north wall. All the paths to Olivet converge at the ancient road which winds down the steep bank to the bridge. I always felt, as I passed down that road and crossed the Kidron, that I was treading in the very footsteps of my Lord, and on that very path along which he so often retired, weary and sorrowful, to his retreat in Gethsemane.

After crossing the bridge, the ancient road ascends the lower slope of Olivet for about a hundred yards, and then branches. One branch runs right up to the summit, the other turns to the right. In the angle between them is a little garden, enclosed by a high modern wall. This is the *traditional*, and it may be the *real* GETHSEMANE. At anyrate, Gethsemane could not have been far distant. The garden belongs to the Latin convent. Entering, we find trim flower-beds, and gravel walks. These have no attractions for us; neither has "the bank on which the apostles slept," nor "the Grotto of the Agony," nor any other of the apocryphal "holy places," which ecclesiastical superstition has located there; but eight venerable olive-trees rivet our attention. They are real patriarchs; their huge trunks are rent, hollowed, gnarled, and propped up, and their boughs hoary with age. They seem old enough, and probably *are* old enough, to have formed an arbour for Jesus. How often have I sat on a rocky bank in that garden! How often, beneath the grateful shade of the old olives, have I read and re-read the story of the betrayal! How often have I fondly lingered there far on into the still night, when the city above was hushed in sleep, and no sound was heard save the sighing of the breeze among the olive branches, thinking and thinking on those miracles of love and power that He performed there!

> "Who can thy deep wonders see,
>   Wonderful Gethsemane!
> There my God bare all my guilt—
>   This through grace can be believed;
> But the horrors which he felt
>   Are too vast to be conceived.
> None can penetrate through thee,
> Doleful, dark Gethsemane!"

*John xviii. 2.

The Destruction of the Temple foretold.—Our Lord had paid his last visit to the Temple. When passing out, solemn and sad, the disciples said, "Master, see what manner of stones and what buildings are here!" They had probably heard some word fall from his lips which excited their alarm, and they thus tried to awaken in his mind a deeper interest in their venerated Temple. It was in vain. "Seest thou these great buildings? there shall not be left one stone upon another, that shall not be thrown down."* He went on, crossed the Kidron, and followed the road to Bethany; apparently the lower road, for he came to a commanding point "over against the Temple," and there sat down. The Temple and its courts were in full view; the eye could see distinctly across the ravine the gorgeous details of its architecture, and the colossal magnitude of its masonry; and there, with his eye upon them, and his disciples' attention directed to them, he foretold the destruction of both Temple and City, summing up with the terrible words, "This generation shall not pass away till all be fulfilled. Heaven and earth shall pass away; but my words shall not pass away."†

I walked up that same path. I sat down on a projecting rock "over against the Temple." It may not have been the very spot on which Christ sat, but it could not have been far from it. I looked, and I saw that the prophecy was fulfilled to the letter—not a single stone of the Temple remains. I read the whole of the prophecies and parables uttered at that place by the Saviour, and I read them with a far deeper interest, and a far more intense feeling of reality than I had ever experienced before.‡

David's Flight from Absalom.—Crossing the Kidron by the bridge—a bridge which, I may state, is only intended to raise the road, as there is neither "brook" nor brook-bed in this part of the Kidron—leaving the picturesque Church of the Virgin down in its sunken area on the left, and Gethsemane on the right, I climbed the ancient road to the top of Olivet. Here and there the rock has been cut away, and rude steps formed; more frequently deep tracks or channels, worn by the feet of countless wayfarers during long, long centuries, are seen on the rocky ledges. I was now in the footsteps of David, who, when fleeing from Absalom, "went over the brook Kidron toward *the way of the wilderness*....and went up by the ascent of Olivet, and wept as he went up, and had his head covered; and he went barefoot; and all the people that was with him covered every man his head, and they went up weeping as they went."§ It was a sad and touching spectacle; and dearly did the king then pay for those sins which had led to the formation of an ill-assorted and badly-trained family.

On reaching the top of the mount, David turned to take a last fond look at his home, now the seat of unnatural rebellion; and there, in sight of the Holy City and the Ark, he paused to worship God. In his hour of suffering he carried into practice the noble sentiments

---

*Mark xiii. 1, 2.   †Luke xxi. 33.   ‡Matt. xxiv.-xxvi.   §2 Sam. xv. 23, 30.

of the Forty-second Psalm: "I will say unto God my rock, Why hast thou forgotten me? why go I mourning because of the oppression of the enemy?....Why art thou cast down, O my soul? and why art thou disquieted within me? hope thou in God; for I shall yet praise him, who is the health of my countenance, and my God." From the brow of Olivet the eye looks down upon Jerusalem as upon an embossed picture. The ravines that surround it, the walls that encompass it, the streets and lanes that zigzag through it, are all visible. From the same spot another and a widely

BETHANY.

different view opens to the eastward. The mount stands on the edge of the wilderness. With the crowded city behind, and the bare parched desert in front, one would almost think Olivet divided the living from the dead. The "wilderness of Judea" begins at our feet, breaking down in a succession of white naked hills, and jagged limestone cliffs, and bare gray ravines, until at length the hills drop suddenly and precipitously into the deep valley of the Jordan; beyond which rises, as suddenly and precipitously, an unbroken mountain range extending north and south along the horizon, far as the eye can see. That range is the *Peræa,* the "place beyond," of the New Testament, and the Moab and Gilead of the Old. The "way" along which David fled was appropriately named the "way of the wilderness." That "wilderness" was the scene of the Temptation; and the "way" through it was the scene of the parable of the Good Samaritan, which was related by our Lord either upon this very summit, or on the path between it and Bethany. How doubly striking must that beautiful illustration of charity have been when Jesus would point to that dreary, dangerous desert road, while repeating the words, "A certain man went down from Jerusalem to Jericho, and fell among thieves"!*

The Ascension.—"And he led them out as far as to Bethany, and he lifted up his hands and blessed them; and it came to pass, while he blessed them, he was parted from them, and carried up into heaven."† When on Olivet I was deeply impressed with the belief—I can scarcely tell why, but so it was—that Jesus on this occasion took the upper road, over the top of the mount. It was more private; and the moment the summit was passed, he and his disciples were in absolute solitude. Jerusalem is shut out by the hill, and Bethany is hidden until we reach a rocky spur overhanging the little nook in which it lies embosomed. "He led them out *as far as* to Bethany." This can scarcely mean into Bethany. The Ascension appears to have been witnessed only by the disciples, and it could not therefore have taken place *in* the village; but it must have been close to it. I saw one spot, "as far" from Jerusalem as Bethany, very near the village, and yet concealed from view, and I thought that it in all probability was the very place on which the Saviour's feet last rested. As I sat there, and read the simple, graphic story of the Ascension,‡ I was impressed as I never had been before with the intense, the almost startling vividness of the sacred narrative:—The Saviour gradually ascending while the words of blessing flowed from his lips—the wondering, awe-stricken disciples following him upward and upward with eager gaze—the cloud slowly folding round him, and at length hiding him in its bright bosom—the white-robed angels bursting suddenly from it and standing in the midst of the disciples! What a glorious picture! What joy it brings to the Christian's heart! Our Substitute, our Saviour, our Brother, our Forerunner, thus ascending on the wings of victory to the heaven he had won for us! While I read and meditated, it seemed as if there was wafted to my ear in voice of sweetest melody the cheering sound of the angelic promise, "This same Jesus, which is taken up from you into heaven, shall so come in like manner as ye have seen him go into heaven."§ "Even so, come, Lord Jesus."

*Luke x. 25-37.   †Luke xxiv. 50.   ‡Luke xxiv. 50; Acts i. 9-12.   §Acts i. 11.

The top of the Mount of Olives is the traditional scene of the Ascension, and a church was built over it in the fourth century, by Helena, the mother of Constantine. That building has long since disappeared, and the reputed site is now occupied by a humble chapel which stands in the court of a mosque! Crowds of pilgrims visit it, and have done so for many centuries. The guardian shows them the print of one of the Saviour's feet in the rock, and tells them that both footprints were there until the Mohammedans stole one of them. Bishop Ellicott and others think the traditional may be the true site of the Ascension; but I cannot see how the words "as far as to Bethany" can be made to signify, to the top of Olivet, which is not half-way to that village.

Bethany.—What particularly struck me in all my visits to Bethany was its solitude. It looks as if it were shut out from the whole world. No town, village, or human habitation is visible from it. The wilderness appears in front through an opening in the rocky glen, and the steep side of Olivet rises close behind. When Jesus retired from Jerusalem to Bethany, no sound of the busy world followed him—no noisy crowd broke in upon his meditation. In the quiet home of Martha, or in some lonely recess of Bethany's secluded dell, he rested, and taught, and prayed. How delighted I was one evening, when seated on a rocky bank beside the village, reading the story of Lazarus, to hear a passing villager say, "There is the tomb of Lazarus, and yonder is the house of Martha!" They may not be, most probably they are not, the real places; but this is Bethany, and the miracle wrought there still dwells in the memory of its inhabitants. And when the unvarying features of nature are there too—the cliffs, the secluded glen, the Mount of Olives—few will think of traditional "holy places." From the place where I sat I saw—as Martha and Mary had seen from their house-top—those blue mountains beyond Jordan, where Jesus was abiding when they sent unto him, saying, "Lord, behold, he whom thou lovest is sick."* I saw the road "from Jerusalem to Jericho" winding past the village, and away down the rocky declivities into the wilderness. By that road Jesus was expected, and one can fancy with what earnest, longing eyes, the sisters looked along it, ever and anon returning and looking, from the first dawn till waning twilight. And when at last he did come, and Martha heard the news, one can picture the touching scene—how she ran along that road, and with streaming eyes and quivering lips uttered the half-reproachful and still half-hopeful cry, "Lord, if thou hadst been here my brother had not died."

Bethany is now, and apparently always was, a small, poor, mountain hamlet, with nothing to charm except its seclusion, and nothing to interest save its associations. It is a remarkable fact that Christ's great miracle has been to it as a new baptism, conferring a new name. It is now called *El-Azarîyeh*; which may be interpreted, "The Place of Lazarus." The "palms" are all gone which gave it the old name *Beth-any*, "House of

---

*John x. 40; xi. 3.

Dates;" but the crags around and the terraced slopes above it are dotted yet with venerable fig-trees, as if to show that its sister village, *Beth-phage*, "House of Figs," is not forgotten, though its site is lost. The houses of Bethany are of stone, massive and rude in style. Over them, on the top of a scarped rock, rises a fragment of heavy ancient masonry—perhaps a portion of an old watch-tower. The reputed tomb of Lazarus is a deep, narrow vault, apparently of no great antiquity.

Christ's Triumphal Entry into Jerusalem.—Our Lord reached Bethany from Jericho on the evening of Friday, after sunset, or the morning of Saturday, the Jewish Sabbath;* and on the next day† he made his triumphal entry into Jerusalem. It was the Passover week. The Holy City was crowded, and the fame of Jesus, and of the miracle he had performed on Lazarus, brought multitudes to Bethany. He knew that the time was come for the complete fulfilment of prophecy, and that Zion's King should that day in triumph enter Zion's gates. Knowing what was before him, it was natural he should take the easy caravan road round the southern shoulder of Olivet, and not the steep and difficult one over the summit. When setting forth, there was nothing either in dress or mien to distinguish Jesus from others. Prophecy declared that he should be "meek and lowly," and he was "meek and lowly." The little band of humble disciples gathered closely round his person, while the multitude thronged the path and lined the rocky banks above it. Soon after leaving Bethany the road meets a ravine which furrows deeply the side of Olivet. From this point the top of Zion is seen, but the rest of the city is hid by an intervening ridge; and just opposite this point, on the other side of the ravine, I saw the site and remains of an ancient village. The road turns sharply to the right, descends obliquely to the bottom of the ravine, and then turning to the left, ascends and reaches the top of the opposite ridge a short distance above the site of the village. Is not this the place where Jesus said to the two disciples, *"Go into the village over against you"?* These active footmen could cross the ravine direct in a minute or two, while the great procession would take some time in slowly winding round the road. The people of the village saw the procession; they knew its cause, for the fame of Jesus' miracles had reached them; they were thus prepared to give the ass to the disciples the moment they heard, "The Lord hath need of him." And the disciples, taking the ass, led it up to the road, and met Jesus. A temporary saddle was soon made of the loose outer robes of the people, as I have myself seen done a hundred times in Palestine. Some of the people now broke down branches from the palm-trees, and waving them in triumph, threw them in the path. Others, still more enthusiastic, spread their garments in the way, as I have seen Mohammedan devotees do before a distinguished saint. Zechariah's prophecy was fulfilled to the letter: "Rejoice greatly, O daughter of Zion; shout, O daughter of

---

*John xii. 1.   †John xii. 12.

AIN KARIM.

This page is adjacent to a plate and is intentionally left blank.

Jerusalem: behold, thy King cometh unto thee: he is just, and having salvation; lowly, and riding upon an ass."*

The procession advances. The crown of the ridge is gained, and Jerusalem in its full extent and beauty bursts upon the view. Moriah, crowned by the Temple, rises proudly from the deep, dark Kidron; Zion rises higher yet away beyond it, showing to advantage the Palace of Herod, and the lofty battlements of Hippicus and its sister towers; then the great City, and its gardens stretching far beyond. One look on their beloved and beauteous City, and one on their wonder-working King†, the multitudes raise their voices in a long shout of triumph: "Hosanna to the son of David; blessed is he that cometh in the name of the Lord; hosanna in the highest."‡

But how was Jesus affected by these joyous acclamations and by that noble view? His omniscient eye looked beneath the exuberance of enthusiasm in upon the evil heart of unbelief. It looked, too, from the gorgeous buildings of the city, away down the dark vista of time, and saw looming in the future, ruin, desolation, and woe. Therefore when he came near,—when he came down probably to that point where the Temple was directly facing him, and all the richness of its architecture could be seen,—"He wept over it:"—

"Why doth my Saviour weep
   At sight of Sion's bowers?
Shows it not fair from yonder steep,
   Her gorgeous crown of towers?
Mark well his holy pains;
   'Tis not in pride or scorn
That Israel's King with sorrow stains
   His own triumphal morn.

"'If thou hadst known, e'en thou,
   At least in this thy day,
The message of thy peace! but now
   'Tis passed for aye away:
Now foes shall trench thee round,
   And lay thee even with earth,
And dash thy children to the ground,
   Thy glory and thy mirth.'

"And doth the Saviour weep
   Over his people's sin,
Because we will not let him keep
   The souls he died to win?
Ye hearts that love the Lord,
   If at this sight ye burn,
See that in thought, in deed, in word,
   Ye hate what made him mourn."

The scene here closes, so far as Olivet is concerned. The mount is studded all over with traditional "holy places," but the only ones which tend to illustrate the sacred narrative, or throw light on the journeys, parables, prophecies, and miracles of our Lord, are those to which I have conducted my reader.

*Zech. ix. 9.   †Luke xix. 37.   ‡Matt. xxi. 9.

AIN KARIM: THE CONVENT OF ST. JOHN THE BAPTIST.

AN excursion to Ain Karim, the village and Convent of St. John, forms a pleasant ride from the Holy City. The distance is about four miles, and the road leads over the table-land to the west, affording commanding views of the country northward to Mizpeh, distinguished by its tall minaret; southward over the little upland plain of Rephaim to Bethlehem; and westward among a network of dark glens, with conical hills between, each crowned with village or ruin. We reach the brow of the great valley of Beit Hanina, the traditional, but many miles distant from the real, *Elah*. The village of Ain Karim now comes into view below us on the eastern slope of the valley, surrounded by well-kept and luxuriant vineyards and olive-groves. Beside it we also notice a trim enclosed garden, studded with cypresses.

It is a thriving village, chiefly owing to the influence and praiseworthy exertions of the monks, who, in addition to conducting useful elementary schools, instruct the people in the proper cultivation of their fields. The beneficial effects are visible on every side, and one sees here what the rugged hills of Palestine might be made by industry, enterprise, and skill.

On a raised site in the centre of the village stands the *Franciscan Convent of St. John in the Desert*. Its church is large and handsome. It includes the traditional site of the house of Zacharias, in which the Baptist was born. The place of birth is a grotto, like so many other holy places in this land, and is richly adorned with marble, bas-reliefs, and paintings. In the centre of the pavement is a slab with the following inscription:—

HIC PRÆCURSOR DOMINI NATUS EST.
("Here the Forerunner of the Lord was born.")

About a mile distant, on the slope of a hill, is the site of the country house of Zacharias. Tradition says that the Virgin Mary on her visit went first to Elizabeth's village-residence, but not finding her there, she proceeded to that in the country; and there took place the interview narrated by the evangelist.*

*Luke i. 39-45.

BETHLEHEM.

IN sacred interest *Bethlehem*, though it be "little among the thousands of Judah," is only second to Jerusalem itself. Its name is a household word throughout Christendom. It is one of those Scripture sites concerning whose identity there never was, and there never can be, any doubt or controversy. The modern name *Beit-Lahm*, "House of Flesh," is somewhat different in sound and meaning from the ancient Hebrew *Beth-Lehem*, "House of Bread;" but it is doubtless a popular corruption, such as one frequently meets with in Palestine. In olden times the town was called Beth-lehem Judah, to distinguish it from another Beth-lehem in Zebulun.* It was also called *Ephratah*, "the Fruitful;"† probably for the same reason that the name "House of Bread" had been given to it. It is encompassed by ground which, though rugged and rocky, is yet carefully cultivated, and rich in corn, vineyards, and olive-groves. There is also now, as there was in David's time, a wide and wild region of pasture land, reaching away down through the wilderness of Judah to "the rocks of the wild goats" at En-gedi on the shore of the Dead Sea.‡

I have again and again approached Bethlehem with feelings of deepest interest,—almost of awe. With the Bible in my hand, stirring memories of the long distant past came up on each visit fresh before me; and names, familiar to the mountain shepherds whom I met, helped me to localize many an incident of Scripture history. I have climbed the precipitous path leading up to it from the Convent of St. Saba, on the way to Jericho; and from the Cave of Adullam in the gloomy ravine of Khureitûn; and from the conical peak of the Frank Mountain, where Herod had a fortress, and where he was buried;—I have ridden to it over the bare hill-tops from the deserted ruins of Tekoa; and I have pursued more than once the well-beaten pilgrim path from Jerusalem,—and found something new, and fresh, and instructive in every view I got. I shall now try to give my readers a few pictures by pen and pencil of what I saw.

In going from Jerusalem to Bethlehem one leaves by the Jaffa Gate, crosses the upper part of the Valley of Hinnom, looking down into the Lower Pool of Gihon, and up beyond it to the neat cottages built by Sir Moses Montefiore for poor Jews. On reaching the brow of the hill south of Hinnom, it is well to turn round and take a look at the Holy City. The hills and valleys are here seen to greater advantage than from any other point. The deepest parts of Hinnom, Tyropœon, and Kidron are nearest us; and Zion, Moriah, and Olivet stand out prominently.

*Joshua xix. 15. †Micah v. 2. ‡1 Sam. xxiv. 1, 2.

We pass on, and a gentle descent over stony ground brings us into the little plain of Rephaim, "the valley of the giants," as travellers call it, and as it is named in the Book of Joshua.* It was here David gained some of his most signal victories over the Philistines.† The plain is about a mile long, and descends on the west to a pleasant glen filled with roses, where the enthusiastic pilgrim may visit the Fountain of Yalo, overhung by the ruins of a chapel of some unknown age. Tradition makes it the scene of the baptism of the Ethiopian eunuch, and names it Philip's Fountain. The position does not answer to the apostolic narrative. There can be no doubt, however, that it is on the ancient road from Jerusalem to Gaza.

RACHEL'S TOMB—BETHLEHEM BEYOND.

Proceeding over the plain of Rephaim, along the broad path, my attention was called to a well, which I found to be another traditional Scripture site. The story is, that the "wise men from the east," when dismissed by Herod, proceeded thus far in uncertainty. Stooping, however, according to the custom of thirsty travellers, to draw water, they suddenly saw their guiding star mirrored in the well. The tradition, if it has no other claim upon our attention, reminds us that along this very path the Magi travelled from the court of Herod to the NEW-BORN KING in Bethlehem.

A few minutes more takes us up a rocky slope to the Convent of Elias, where, we are told, the great prophet lay down under the shade of an olive-tree, weary, hungry, and

---

*Joshua xv. 8.   †2 Sam. v. 18-25.

careworn, when he fled from the infamous Jezebel. On the surface of the smooth rock, just in front of the convent gate, is a slight depression, said to be that left by the prophet where he slept.

Here the Tomb of Rachel, with Bethlehem beyond, and the bleak hills of Judea in the background, suddenly bursts upon the view. The tomb is still half-a-mile distant, and Bethlehem a mile beyond; but in the clear atmosphere they are seen with great distinctness, and our natural inclination is to hasten forward and rest beside the tomb. On approaching it, we observe on the right the village of Beit Jala, with some imposing new buildings beside it. It is the Zelzah mentioned by Samuel, when sending Saul home after anointing him king at Ramah. Saul had followed the path we have taken, after passing Jerusalem; and the words of the prophet are now called up to our mind: "When thou art departed from me to-day, then thou shalt find two men by Rachel's sepulchre, in the border of Benjamin, at Zelzah,"* etc. One is struck everywhere, in wandering through Palestine, with the minute accuracy of the topographical notices of the sacred writers. Here is the sepulchre of Rachel, and there near us is Zelzah, retaining its ancient name, only in an Arabic form.

The *"Sepulchre of Rachel"* is a modern building, a small dome surmounting a square chamber at one end, and nothing particular in form or material in any part of it. The tomb was probably a natural cave, and may be underneath. The identity of the site cannot be questioned. It is one of the few shrines which Muslems, Jews, and Christians agree in honouring, and about which their traditions are identical. There is much of simple pathos in the Bible narrative, which will be read on the spot, or even with a faithful picture before one, with new and fresh interest: "And they journeyed from Beth-el; and there was still some way to come to Ephrath...And Rachel died, and was buried in the way to Ephrath (the same is Beth-lehem). And Jacob set up a pillar upon her grave: the same is the pillar of Rachel's grave unto this day."† The pillar was still there when Moses wrote the narrative in the Book of Genesis. It has long since been swept away; but thirty centuries of sorrow and suffering have not been able to sweep away the memory of it from the hearts of Rachel's posterity. The monument is there yet, retaining the name of the patriarch's beloved wife. Bethlehem is there beyond it, and the main features of the scene are there, as when Jacob passed on mourning. It is on the border too, we are told, of the territory subsequently allotted to the tribe of Benjamin, the descendants of him whom his mother named, with her last breath, on this spot, *Ben-oni*, "Son of my sorrow."

Another touching incident is recalled by Rachel's Sepulchre. When Herod "slew all the male children that were in Bethlehem, and in all the borders thereof, from two years old and under...then was fulfilled that which was spoken by Jeremiah the prophet,

*1 Sam. x. 2.   †Gen. xxxv. 16-20.

saying, A voice was heard in Ramah, weeping and great mourning, Rachel weeping for her children."* The territory of Benjamin adjoined Judah at Rachel's Sepulchre, and a section of the former was included in the massacre. Therefore, in the poetic imagery of the East, Rachel is represented as rising from her tomb and weeping over her slaughtered children.

Bethlehem is now before us, standing on a narrow ridge which projects eastward from the central range of the hills of Judah, and breaks down in terraced slopes to deep glens on the north and south, and to a broad reach of table-land on the east. The terraces are covered with

BETHLEHEM.

vineyards and studded with olives; they sweep round the ridge regular as steps of stairs. On the eastern brow of the ridge, separated from the crowded village by an open esplanade, is the convent, like a large, feudal castle. It is a huge pile, consisting of the Church of the Nativity and the three convents—Latin, Greek, and Armenian—abutting on its north, east, and south sides.

The site is most commanding, the view from it embracing a large section of the

*Matt. ii. 16-18.

Church and Convent, Bethlehem.

This page is adjacent to a plate and is intentionally left blank.

wilderness of Judea, the Jordan valley and Dead Sea, and the purple-tinted mountain-chain of Moab and Gilead stretching like a great wall along the horizon, north and south, far as the eye can see.

At our feet, as we stand on the terraced roof, are the fields, the scene of the romantic story of Ruth and Boaz. Beyond them, one of the reverend fathers will point out the spot, on the border of the wilderness, where the shepherds were abiding with their flocks by night, when "the angel of the Lord stood by them, and the glory of the Lord shone round about them…And the angel said unto them, Behold, I bring you good tidings of great joy, which shall be to all the

THE SHEPHERDS' FIELDS, BETHLEHEM.

people."* From that spot the "good tidings"—the God *spell*, the GOSPEL—were borne far and wide, until, in our day, they sweep round the Earth. In Bethlehem, looking out on that upland plain, we seem to realize the first outburst of the heavenly message, and to feel more intensely its inspiring power.

Other stirring memories of Bethlehem's eventful history rise before us:—The advent of the prophet Samuel to the house of Jesse the Bethlehemite; his sending to the wilderness to bring the stripling David from tending his sheep, and the anointing him king of Israel; the subsequent troubled life and startling adventures of the shepherd monarch:

*Luke ii. 9, 10.

how he defied and defeated the Philistine hosts that encompassed his native town; how a chosen band of three active shepherd warriors exposed their lives in a successful raid to gratify his singular wish: "Oh that one would give me water to drink of the well of Beth-lehem, which is by the gate!"* The well is there, a few hundred yards along the road leading to Jerusalem. We can see it from the convent; and we can trace the probable route taken by the courageous shepherds up from the Cave of Adullam, away down in that dark wild ravine to the right, through the more exposed vineyards immediately below us, then up the little side glen on the left, and breaking boldly through the Philistine guards, drawing water and carrying it off in triumph to their leader. The simple yet graphic narrative assumes the vividness of a life-scene as we read it on the old stage.

Another and far more momentous sacred drama was enacted in the region now before our eyes. The dark line of foliage that marks the course of the Jordan is seen away in the bottom of that great valley. The wilderness—naked, rugged, utterly desolate—extends from beside the vineyards of Bethlehem to the cliffs that hem in the Jordan valley. How wonderfully expressive here appears to us every phrase in St. Matthew's narrative of THE TEMPTATION. It is well to read it again on the spot, or at least with the leading features of the scene before the mind's eye, and to emphasize each descriptive term and expression.

"Then was Jesus led *up* of the Spirit into *the wilderness* to be tempted of the devil. And when he had *fasted* forty days and forty nights, he afterward hungered. And the tempter came and said unto him, If thou art the Son of God, command that *these stones* become *loaves*."† The surface of that wilderness is covered with rounded flakes of whitish limestone, resembling in form and colour the ordinary loaves of bread then, as now, in common use. Jesus "fasted." There was nothing there for him to eat. He was alone. There were then, and there are now, no human habitations in the wilderness. In one of those graphic touches which St. Mark occasionally gives to gospel history, we read, "He was with the wild beasts."‡ The leopard, the bear, the hyena, and the prowling wolf and jackal, infest the wilderness at the present day, as did the lion and the bear§ when David kept his father's sheep, and showed the courage and prowess which afterwards marked his whole career.

We leave the terraced roof of the convent, from which such a wide and interesting view is obtained, and we descend to the open court outside, where the whole of the massive buildings are before us. Their great strength, the small dimensions of the doors and windows, the height of the walls, and the general aspect, show only too plainly that the structure was intended for defence as well as for divine worship. Like many another convent and church in Palestine, it has been the scene of strife and bloodshed. Bethlehem

*2 Sam. xxiii. 15. †Matt. iv. 1-3. ‡Mark i. 13. §1 Sam. xvii. 34.

is now inhabited exclusively by Christians; but it is surrounded by turbulent and fanatical Muslems—villagers who till the soil, and Bedawin who dwell in tents and feed their sheep and goats in the wilderness, and steal.

The men of Bethlehem are strong, industrious, and brave. They cultivate their fields and vineyards and olive-groves with care and success. The women are fairer in complexion and more graceful in carriage and manner than any others of the native population of southern Palestine. There may be among them some of the descendants of the Crusaders who, we are

BEAD-SELLERS, BETHLEHEM.

told, settled in the village. Like all women of the East, they are fond of personal ornaments, and generally wear, even the lowest classes among them, a profusion of bracelets, necklaces, and even in some cases nose-jewels.

Entering an inner court, we find the venders of beads and other trinkets squatting, Arab fashion, on the stone pavement, plying their trade just as the Jews were wont to do in former ages in the outer court of the Temple. The carving of beads, crucifixes, models of the Cave of the Nativity and of the Holy Sepulchre, in olive-wood, mother-of-pearl, and bituminous limestone from the Dead Sea, has for centuries been one of the staple trades of the Bethlehemites. Some of them are chaste in design and delicate in workmanship; others are rough and rude; but they all command a ready sale from pilgrims and travellers. I have seen imposing shops in leading cities of England and Scotland filled with carved work of nearly every description—boxes, paper-knives, picture-frames, ink-stands, and many other articles—all the products of the industrious men and women of Bethlehem. Work in nacre, or mother-of-pearl, is one of the leading industries. Leonardo da Vinci's picture of "The Last Supper" is their favourite subject, and it is exposed for sale carved on shells and olive-wood, sometimes executed with considerable skill. The figure here given, with the intelligent face, voluminous turban, and graceful flowing robes, is a native artist in nacre-work.

WORKER IN NACRE, BETHLEHEM.

The Church of the Nativity is a basilica, erected by the Empress Helena in A.D. 327, and is therefore the oldest existing monument of Christian architecture in the world. It is one hundred and twenty feet long by one hundred and ten wide; and is divided, by ranges of Corinthian columns, into central nave and four aisles. The columns are marble, and were probably taken from the porches of Herod's Temple. This is the only part of the building of any architectural interest.

The arrangement of the choir is peculiar, owing to the crypt beneath it being the great object of attraction to Christian pilgrims. It is separated from the nave by a dead, unsightly wall, and is divided into two chapels—one Greek, the other Armenian; from each a staircase leads down to the Grotto of the Nativity. On the north side of the choir is the Latin Church of St. Catherine; and from it there is also a passage down to the Grotto.

The Grotto and Study of St. Jerome is among the most interesting spots in Bethlehem. It has this great advantage, too, that it is authentic. It is reached by a winding, narrow, subterranean passage from the Latin Church. I entered it with no little emotion. It is a small square vault, hewn in the rock, with a raised dais of rock round it. On the eastern side is an altar, and an old faded painting above it, representing the saint writing and the lion at his side. "Here it was that the illustrious recluse passed a great portion of his life; and here it was that he produced those laborious works which have justly

INTERIOR OF THE CHURCH OF THE NATIVITY.

earned him the title of the 'Father of the Church.'" This is the veritable study of St. Jerome—the spot which the Biblical scholar and ecclesiastical historian will regard with peculiar interest. Here the Holy Scriptures were translated into Latin—that Latin version, that VULGATE, which now for fourteen centuries has been the acknowledged standard in the Roman Catholic Church.

The Chapel of the Nativity.—The Grotto of the Nativity appears to have been honoured as early as the second century, and is thus probably the very oldest of the *holy caves* of Palestine. It is a low, somewhat irregular vault, apparently hewn in the rock, thirty-eight feet long by eleven wide. At the east end is a semicircular apse, the sanctum of the entire structure—convent, churches, and chapels. On a marble slab fixed in the pavement, with a silver star in the centre, are these words:—

> HIC DE VIRGINE MARIA JESUS CHRISTUS NATUS EST.
> ("Here Jesus Christ was born of the Virgin Mary.")

Not far distant, in an angle of the Grotto, is the *Chapel of the Manger*. But the real manger is gone. It was, we are told, carried to Rome and deposited in the grand basilica of Santa Maria Maggiore. In its place here is a trough of white marble.

These various grottoes and sanctuaries and altars are minutely measured off and distributed among the rival Christian sects—Latins, Greeks, and Armenians. Many a bitter contest has there been among them for a few inches of a wall, or for the fraction of an altar. And more than once the question of the opening of a door, or the closing of a staircase, or the precedence of an officiating monk, has well-nigh involved Europe in war.

There are numerous other holy places within the walls—the Altar of the Innocents, the Chapel of Joseph, the Station of the Wise Men, and so forth; but the mere mention of them is enough, and we ascend to the splendid basilica, and pass out to the free, open air.

This is Bethlehem, the city of David, the birth-place of our Lord. Its natural features remain as they were when David kept his father's sheep in the adjoining desert; when the Eastern Magi came from Jerusalem to see the NEW-BORN KING; and when the shepherds heard the angelic host proclaiming, "Glory to God in the highest, and on earth peace, good will toward men." The inhabitants, too, have probably the same characteristics—active, fearless, and restless.

Passing through the open esplanade, the usual market-place, we observe groups of women, neatly dressed in their picturesque Eastern costumes, and almost covered with ornaments. Here, as elsewhere in Syria, the women carry their fortunes on their heads, necks, arms, and girdles. They have long strings of coins, ancient and modern, gold and silver, ranged over their foreheads, and hanging down on each side of the face; they have bands of coins round the plaited hair, sometimes round the waist. They have large

*Luke ii. 13.

WOMEN OF BETHLEHEM.

This page is adjacent to a plate and is intentionally left blank.

jewelled ear-rings, gold-embroidered jackets, and heavy bracelets and anklets of gold and silver. The full dress of a Syrian maid or matron is very elaborate; and like ladies in more highly civilized countries, the belles of Bethlehem seem to delight in exhibiting their finery. We see a group of them here faithfully represented, sitting in a recess of the market-place, decked in gold and jewels, and with that easy, placid, and graceful mien which characterizes all the women of Bethlehem. The pottery pitcher at their feet is probably, in shape and material, such as Abraham put on poor Hagar's shoulder when he sent her away into the wilderness of Beersheba; and the little jar on the stone overhead is in form a facsimile of one I got out of an ancient Phœnician tomb in Cyprus. Dress, personal ornaments, household utensils, and manners and customs, are all stereotyped in the East. The two bracelets "of ten shekels weight of gold" which Abraham's servant gave to Rebekah at the well of Haran, in Mesopotamia, we could easily match this day at the well of Bethlehem.

This town was a place of note in the time of the Crusades. The Christian army, on its approach to Jerusalem, took possession of it, at the earnest request of the inhabitants; and King Baldwin the First made it an episcopal see; but although the Pope confirmed the act, and the title was long retained in the Latin Church, the actual occupancy of the see was of very short continuance.

THE CAVE OF ADULLAM AND THE POOLS OF SOLOMON.

TWO places ought to be visited from Bethlehem—the Cave of Adullam and the Pools of Solomon. They are both within an easy ride; and I shall try to take my readers there in spirit. A visit to Adullam affords views of the desolation and stern grandeur of that wilderness and of those "rocks of the wild goats"* where David and his men found refuge from the troops of Saul, and where they were trained to deeds of daring which they displayed so frequently in after days. There, too, when traversing the mountains, I found it would not be difficult to raise, among the active shepherd Taamirah and the more warlike Jehâlin Arabs, a band that might rival David's followers. He had gathered round him here, in the recesses of his native hills, "every one that was in distress, and every one that was in debt, and every one that was discontented."† There were hundreds of such men around me. In fact this seems to be, to no small extent, the chronic state of the sparse population. In restlessness, cunning, daring, unscrupulous tendency to forays, they are unsurpassed.

*1 Sam. xxiv. 2. †1 Sam. xxii. 2.

In this short excursion, too, one can see, better perhaps than at any other point, the naked, rugged, and utterly desolate aspect of the wilderness in which our Lord spent forty days and forty nights "among the wild beasts," fasting, and tempted of the devil.

Solomon's Pools give us some little insight into the nature and triumphs of Jewish engineering. They here took advantage of a pure and copious mountain spring, stored up with marvellous care and ingenuity its surplus water, overcame great natural obstacles, constructed an aqueduct over hill and dale for about ten miles, and introduced an abundant supply of water into the Holy City and the Temple area. I have traced one old aqueduct through its entire course. It is broken and useless now; but it could, at a comparatively small cost, be repaired. The Turks, however, are not given to repair anything. Ruin follows their footsteps everywhere, and nowhere more conspicuously than in Palestine.

The Cave of Adullam.—We set out for Khureitun: such is the Arab name both of the cave and of the ravine in which it is situated. Just as we leave Bethlehem, we see on the top of a bleak, gray ridge in the far distance, a group of ruins. It is Tekoa, the birth-place of Amos, who was "among the herdmen"* of these mountains. Tekoa was long a town of importance in Judah; but it is now, and has been for ages, an uninhabited waste. So complete has been the overthrow of the buildings, and so bare is the site, that when I went to it, a few years ago, I could find no shade in which to sit while I took my hasty mid-day meal. Its ruins are strewed far and wide over the broad top of one of the highest hills in the Judean range. The view from it is magnificent. On the west is seen the whole sweep of the range from Mizpeh to Hebron. On the east lie the wilderness and the Dead Sea. Beyond the Sea and the Jordan is the unbroken chain of Moab and Gilead. On the north is Bethlehem. Below it, nearer us, is the wild ravine of Khureitun, in the bottom of which, two miles distant, is Adullam. To the south is the mountain range running on to Maon and the conical tell of Carmel. It is such a panorama as, once seen, can never be forgotten. It recalls David, and Amos, and the wise woman whom Joab brought to teach David a lesson of humanity.†

We resume our route to Adullam. Riding down a steep, rocky, break-neck path, through terraced vineyards and miniature corn-fields, we reach the bottom of the Valley of Urtas. Our Taamirah guides here join us, for without them the glen could not be safely traversed, nor the caves safely explored. They are a semi-nomad tribe, living partly in tents and partly in fixed huts. Most are shepherds, but a number cultivate patches of ground. They are neither *Bedawin* nor *Fellahin*—as a body they are neither wandering shepherds nor settled cultivators of the soil. They have many of the vices of both, and few of the good qualities of either. They are noted thieves, and make a boast

*Amos i. 1. †2 Sam. xiv. 1-24.

of their dexterity in appropriating the movable property of their neighbours. In appearance they are rather heavy and stolid, wanting in that quick motion, and restless, fiery glance, which characterize most of the desert tribes. Their dress also is generally that of a peasant rather than a son of the desert—a small turban, instead of the *kufiyeh* or kerchief, bound by a fillet of

TAAMIRAH ARABS.

camel's hair. They wear, however, the wide, flowing Arab *abeih* or cloak. They have strength of body and great power of enduring fatigue. They bound along from rock to rock, and seem to delight in clambering up and down the most rugged banks and cliffs.

The glen, at first wide, gradually contracts, its sides rise higher and higher, and at length it becomes like a huge fissure in the mountain. The bottom is encumbered with fragments of fallen rock, which soon block up the path. We come to the ruins of some buildings of a very ancient type; and about a hundred yards farther is the *cave*. The door is in the face of a cliff, and the only approach is along a ledge, across which a portion of the rock has fallen, almost barring the passage. Clambering over this we reach the entrance, a low, narrow door, so narrow that a full-grown man finds difficulty in getting through it. A gallery ten yards long leads into a vast hall, the sides and roof of the rough natural rock. It is one hundred and twenty feet long, and about forty wide, but irregular, having projections and long recesses. It would easily contain seven hundred men. The dimensions of this grand natural cavern can only be seen by lighting it up, as I did, with candles and torches. The effect is fine. The sharp projections along the sides, and the arches and pendants of the lofty roof, remind one of an immense Gothic hall. Narrow passages branch off in all directions, but most of them soon terminate. One, however, runs on for fifty yards or more, to the side of a pit about ten feet deep. Down this I dropped, and went along another passage, low, narrow, dusty, and swarming with bats. It leads to a large chamber, which seems to be the end of the cave, though the Arabs affirm that there is a passage on to Tekoa and Hebron. Here on the white walls are inscribed the names of such as have ventured so far into it. Among them I read with surprise the name of a lady friend. I cannot recommend other ladies, however, to attempt such an exploit. The chief natural attraction of the cave is the hall near the entrance.

The cave has been regarded, by a monastic tradition reaching back to the time of the Crusades, as the Adullam in which David took refuge after his romantic adventure at Gath.* In a country which abounds in caves, it may be rash to select one, without any very definite data, and assert it to be that referred to in Scripture. There cannot be a doubt, however, that this cave, so far as its natural features are concerned, answers well to the narrative. There was a town called Adullam on the borders of Philistia, not far from Gath, but the cave of Adullam may not have been at or near the town of that name. It is not very likely, besides, that David, after his narrow escape, would venture into a cave so close to his enemies. He would be more likely to go to his own country, with every glen and hill and cave in which he was as a shepherd familiar. Other circumstances favour the identity. The wilderness of Judah was David's favourite haunt in every time of threatened peril. It would seem, from the whole narrative, that the Adullam in which he took refuge was not far from Bethlehem; for when his brethren and all his father's house heard he was there, "they went down thither to him." Another incident occurred while David was in the cave which seems to favour this view. He longed for water of the well of Bethlehem, which is by the gate; and three of his "mighty men" broke through the Philistine host which then held Bethlehem, and brought him the water. We also read that from the cave he took his parents across the Jordan, and placed them

*1 Sam. xxii. 1.

with his kinsfolk in Moab. The route hence to Moab is direct, and must always have been safe from Philistine attacks.

On a subsequent occasion we are told David took refuge in the wilderness of En-gedi, and Saul with his army went to seek him "among the rocks of the wild goats." David had then also taken up his quarters in a cave "on the way to En-gedi;" that is, as it seems, the way from Jerusalem. The romantic incidents of that story may be read with a feeling of something like reality at the mouth of this cavern.*

We retrace our steps up the valley, and a little above the junction of the path that leads to Bethlehem we reach the ruins of a very ancient village or town. It is now called Urtas, but the Bible name is Etam.

Etam, or Etham, was built, probably only rebuilt for the purposes of defence, by Rehoboam, along with Bethlehem and Tekoa.† Josephus tells us that Solomon adorned it with gardens and fountains and streams of water, and that from it he conducted the water to Jerusalem. It may perhaps be the same Etam to the top of whose rock Samson retired after his wild acts of revenge upon the Philistines.‡ There is nothing in the romantic story in the Book of Judges to indicate the situation of the rock; but it is not likely that Samson, after making such havock among the Philistines, would take refuge in any place near their country. He would naturally retire into the strongest defiles of his own land. The language of the sacred historian applies well to this wild glen: "Samson *went down* into the cleft of the cliff Etam." The Philistines "*went up*" and invaded Judah. The Israelites asked, "Why are ye come up against us?" The reply was, "To bind Samson." And the men of Judah, with a disgraceful combination of treachery and cowardice, bound Samson hand and foot and gave him up to his enemies. The Philistines raised a shout of triumph when they saw him bound. But their triumph was short-lived. "The Spirit of the Lord came mightily upon" the bound captive. He rent the cords; "and he found a new jaw-bone of an ass, and put forth his hand and took it, and slew a thousand men therewith." Thus Etam recalls to our minds one of the most romantic incidents in Bible history, and one of the most daring and unfortunate of Israel's warriors.

When I last visited Urtas, or Etam, it had recovered some of its ancient richness and beauty. An adventurous Jewish family had settled in it, and by skill and industry had clothed its rocky slopes and bare glen with gardens of fruit and vegetables and fields of corn. It was a pleasant spot; but the bleak hills and rugged cliffs overhead, and the prowling Arabs all around, ever on the watch for a favourable chance to steal, made it wild withal. One cannot get over the feeling of loneliness when he settles down, even for a short time, in such a place. Security, civilization, and peace seem to have gone.

*1 Sam. xxiv.   †2 Chron. xi. 6.   ‡Judges xv.

Nature in her sternest forms encircles us; and man, untutored and untamed, hovering on the borders of his desert home, robs us of all pleasure, and makes life almost a burden.

Solomon's Pools.—A short ride up the glen from Urtas brings us to a basin-shaped depression in the mountain-range, in the bottom of which lie Solomon's Pools. They are partly excavated in the rocky bed of the vale and partly built of large hewn stones. They are three in number, of great size—each being nearly one hundred and fifty yards long, by half as much in breadth, and about forty feet deep. They are so arranged on the natural slope of the ground that the bottom of the upper pool is higher than the surface of the next, the object evidently being to

SOLOMON'S POOLS.

collect and store the greatest possible quantity of water.

The source from which they are supplied is a subterranean fountain some distance above them on the hill-side. The only visible mark of this fountain is an opening like the mouth of a well, generally covered with a large stone. The internal arrangements are very ingenious, and give one the impression that the intention was to conceal the spring. Water in the East is the most valuable treasure. Without it there can be no fertility—indeed, there can be no life. Hence we find that some of the severest struggles the patriarchs had when they roamed over Palestine was for the possession of wells. The opening here leads, at a depth of four yards, to a vaulted chamber, evidently of the highest antiquity. Adjoining this chamber is another. There are four fountains in the chambers, from which the water is carried through a subterranean tunnel to the corner of the upper pool. Here the stream is divided, a portion flowing into a large vault, and thence through a duct into the pool. Another portion of the water, however, is led off, ere it reaches the pool, by an aqueduct, along the hill-side to Bethlehem and Jerusalem. This aqueduct is so constructed that any surplus water can be let off in passing into the second and into the third pool, while a duct joins it from the bottom of the third pool, so as when necessary to give the fullest available supply. The object of this complicated system of springs, vaults, and ducts, was to secure a constant supply of water for Jerusalem. That in ordinary times the water might be as pure as possible, the aqueduct was connected with the fountain-head. When the fountain yielded more than was needed, the surplus passed into the pools in succession. When the supply from the fountain was not sufficient, it was augmented, as required, from the great store in the pools. Another subterranean aqueduct has been discovered which brings, or rather brought in olden times, a further supply to the lower pool, from fountains amid the hills farther south.

  The antiquity of these great reservoirs and of all the annexed engineering works cannot be questioned. Their extent, solidity, and wonderful ingenuity in construction, show that they could only have been executed in times of peace and prosperity. Their distance, too, from Jerusalem, which they were intended to supply with water, proves that the power of the rulers of the city must at the time have been paramount. The fountains were "sealed;" designed to be, when thus enclosed, and to remain in after times, concealed from view and unknown to all invaders. The aqueduct itself, though running over hills and across ravines for some ten miles, is not easily seen by passers by. It is nowhere raised on arches except in crossing the Valley of Hinnom to Zion.

  Strange to say, we find no reference to these gigantic and most useful works in the Bible. That they must have existed during the Jewish monarchy, and when the Temple services were conducted with all their pomp and ceremony, is evident; for in no other way, at least in none hitherto discovered, could a sufficient supply of water have been obtained. Josephus tells us that at Etam, to which Solomon was in the habit of taking a morning drive from his palace, were gardens, and fountains, and streams of water; and Etam, as we have seen, is only a short distance below the Pools. Does not the historic statement of Josephus, connected with the local topography which I have endeavoured to describe, illustrate the striking passage in the Book of Ecclesiastes, where Solomon says, with a display of genuine Oriental boastfulness, "I made me great works...I planted me vineyards: I made me gardens and orchards, and I planted trees in them of all kinds of fruits: I made me pools of water, to water therewith the wood that bringeth forth trees...

So I was great, and increased more than all that were before me in Jerusalem: also my wisdom remained with me"?*

Beside the upper pool is a large building, half castle half caravansary, of Saracenic origin, now occupied by the guardian of the Pools. Near it one generally sees some members, male and female, of the Taamirah tribe. The accompanying engraving is a faithful representation of two of the women, in their loose, flowing desert costume, with their long plaited hair, rings, nose jewels, and large bracelets. The style in which the baby is slung, with a bundle of clothing over the shoulder of the one, and the pipe held in the hand of the other, is quite characteristic of those desert belles. In the background we observe the Saracenic castle, and the Pools near it to the right.

It may be interesting here to give a brief connected account of the several aqueducts which in ancient times brought water to Jerusalem from this region. Josephus informs us that Pontius Pilate offended the Jews by expending the sacred treasures upon an aqueduct by which he brought water to the city from a distance of four hundred furlongs. The aqueduct from Etam already mentioned follows the windings of the hill-sides by Bethlehem to the Valley of Hinnom. On one of the arches on which it crosses the valley is an Arabic inscription informing us that it was built by a certain Prince Melek en-Naser of Egypt; but of course he only repaired it. The date of the inscription is about A.D. 1300. The aqueduct has been traced to the great cisterns beneath the Haram.

Major Wilson's more recent researches have brought to light no less than three ancient aqueducts from the hill country beyond Bethlehem to, or towards, Jerusalem. The first, or low-level aqueduct, he says, "derives its supply of water from three sources: the Pools of Solomon, Ain Etam, and a large reservoir in the Wady Arrub." On leaving the reservoir it "follows a winding course amongst the hills, passing Tekoa, before it reaches Urtas." Its course is below the lower pool. From thence to Jerusalem "it has a serpentine course of thirteen miles, and passes through two tunnels, one under the village of Bethlehem and the other not far from the city." A section of a much older aqueduct, *on the same level*, was discovered by Captain Warren, tunnelled in the rock round the southern brow of Zion. It was evidently of Jewish origin.

The high-level aqueduct derived its supply from several sources among the highlands between Etam and Hebron. The most distant of these has not yet been discovered, but the aqueduct has been traced as far south as Wady Arrub. From that place it is carried along the sides of valleys and through ridges of rock, passing between the upper pool and the "sealed fountain;" the latter of which, as Major Wilson observes, it probably tapped. Thence it runs along the hill-side above Bethlehem and past Rachel's Tomb, near which it crosses a valley in a tube formed of large blocks of stone perforated, cemented together, and embedded in rubble masonry. The tube is fifteen inches in

*Eccles. ii. 4-9.

ARAB WOMEN OF THE TAAMIRAH TRIBE.

This page is adjacent to a plate and is intentionally left blank.

it has not been traced, but it is supposed to have run along the Valley of Rephaim, and to have flowed into a large reservoir lately discovered on the high ground west of the Jaffa Gate of Jerusalem. When excavating for the foundations of the Russian convent, the remains of a very ancient conduit were discovered; and subsequently a section of it was laid bare within the city, at the house of the Latin Patriarch. Major Wilson suggests that this may be the termination of the high-level aqueduct.

"The third aqueduct," says Major Wilson, "was only seen at one place,—to the south of Rachel's Tomb. It was said to follow the northern slope of the ridge lying between Wady Urtas and Wady er-Rahib, and to have done this must have passed under the divide near the head of the Pools by a tunnel."

These particulars of ancient engineering works are most interesting from an antiquarian and also from a scriptural point of view. They give us a clearer insight into the talent and enterprise of the Jews. They show, too, in all probability, something of the character of those "great works" of which Solomon proudly boasts, and upon which the Queen of Sheba looked with profound astonishment. In their engineering, as well as in architecture and art, the Jews may have been instructed by the Phœnicians, whose genius and skill were famed over the world.

Be this as it may, one is always deeply impressed, when travelling through Bible lands, with the minuteness of topographical details, the graphic descriptions of scenery, the vivid sketches of Eastern work, life, character, and costume, given by the sacred writers. Often in a sentence or two a picture is drawn which has the accuracy of a photograph, combined with the rich colouring of a Claude or a Rembrandt. The pictures of David, Samson, Solomon, and John the Baptist, are drawn with a master hand; and when we read the record of their lives and actions on the spot, the old incidents and characters appear to group themselves before the mind's eye. One sees a David in every shepherd in the wilderness of Judah, and a John the Baptist in every Taamirah chief clothed in his cloak of camel's hair with a leathern girdle about his loins.

FROM JERUSALEM TO BETH-EL.

> "I wandered on to many a shrine,
> By faith or history made divine;
> And then I visited each place
> Where valour's deeds had left a trace."

AFTER our pleasant and I trust not uninstructive inspection of the holy shrines in and near Jerusalem, perhaps a passing visit to some of the more stirring scenes of Bible history may gratify my readers. In a circuit of a few miles north of the city, amid the mountains and passes of Benjamin, we see almost at every step some spot famous in olden times;—Mizpeh, the early gathering-place of the tribes; the battle-fields of Gibeon and Beth-horon, where the sun and moon stood still; Beth-el, which preserves to this day in its name, "House of God," a memorial of Jacob's wondrous dream; the mountain top between Bethel and Ai, from which Abraham and Lot viewed the plain of Sodom, and then parted from each other; Ai, the first mountain-fortress captured by the Israelites under Joshua; the ravine of Michmash, famous for the romantic adventure and victory of Jonathan; Anathoth, where the prophet Jeremiah was born; and Nob, from whose conical peak the proud Assyrian conqueror is represented as shaking his hand against Mount Zion. Nowhere in Palestine have we grouped within a limited area so many places of mingled historic and sacred interest. I have before me the record of a visit made years ago. The notes from which it was drawn up were written on each site, and so deep were the impressions then made upon my mind that I feel I can now reproduce them with much of their original freshness.

The stars were still trembling in the sky when, from the top of our little tower on Olivet, we heard the impatient horses champing their bits and our Arab guides talking in deep gutturals at the door beneath. We were soon in the saddle, and dashing down the rocky side of the mount. My companion and dear friend, James Graham, long since gone to his rest and his reward, was a fast and bold horseman, and rode on regardless, apparently, of life and limb. His fiery gray, feeling his master's firm seat and steady hand, leaped from rock to rock and terrace to terrace with the agility and safety of a mountain goat. It was hard to follow such a daring leader on such a path. It was a dewy morn in the end of September, and the air was fresh and balmy. Gethsemane and the Kidron were in deep gloom, but the first fleecy clouds of autumn, high overhead, had already caught the ruddy rays of the coming sun. A death-like silence reigned in the

Holy City as we rode past. Our path led through the olive groves, then across the great northern road, near those huge mounds of ashes which have since given rise to so much learned controversy. At a smart gallop we traversed the rocky table-land at the head of the Kidron valley, where it is little more than a gentle depression, observing, as we passed, the numerous tombs in the rocks on each side. The plain but chaste façade of the Sepulchre of the Judges attracted my special attention. A visit on a later occasion showed me that within its dark vaults are some seventy or eighty recesses for bodies; and here, it is said, the members of the Sanhedrim were laid in state, "every one in his own house."

We had now reached the western brow of the table-land, and the deep glen of Beit Hanina was at our feet, its banks formed into natural terraces by the horizontal strata. The whole scene before us was almost painfully desolate. Verdure there was none. Gray rocks and gray cliffs protruded all around from the gray soil. In places the sides of the glen seemed as if covered with white flags. The few old olives scattered here and there, singly or in little clumps, could scarcely be said to relieve the uniform bareness; for they, too, look dusky and sapless; and the stunted trees and shrubs clinging to the cliffs and hill-sides overhead only serve to make the features of nature more forbidding. There was also a want of colour and variety of outline in the landscape. The dull uniform gray, and the long naked declivities, and the rounded hill-tops had nothing attractive or pleasing in them. Most of the higher hills are singularly formed. They rise in concentric rings of natural terraces from bottom to top.

MIZPEH.

AWAY beyond the glen towered Neby Samwil, the highest and most conspicuous peak in southern Palestine. Its conical top, crowned with village, mosque, and minaret, forms the only striking object in the northern view from Jerusalem. To it we were now bound, as the first point of interest in our excursion. Diving down into the glen, and then clambering up through terraced vineyards, over rude stone fences, along rocky brakes, startling flocks of partridges here and there, at length we gained the summit of the hill. We gave our panting and foaming horses to the care of a group of wild-looking Arab boys who had been watching our approach from the walls of a half-ruined tower. The village sheikh was presently at our side with a welcoming *salâm*, conspicuous in scarlet robe, which now, as in former times, is the badge of royalty or power among the people of Palestine. Several of the village elders stood around him; and their outer garments, in the brilliancy and variety of colour and embroidery, reminded me of Joseph's coat.

Taking the worthy sheikh into our service, we requested him to lead the way to the top of the minaret. What a noble panorama was there! I had seen none to compare with it in extent or interest among the mountains of Palestine. It is far wider than that from Olivet, or Gerizim, or Tabor, or any of the peaks round Hebron. Away on the western horizon slept the "Great Sea;" and from this and other commanding points I was able to understand how natural it was for the ancient Israelite to make the word "sea" (*yam*) a synonym for "west."* Along its glittering shore lay the plains of Sharon and Philistia; the groves of Joppa, looking like the deep

NEBY SAMWIL.

shadow of a cloud; and the towns of Ramleh, Lydda, and Ekron, like points of light on the smooth gray surface. Nearer were the western declivities of Judah's mountain-range, deeply furrowed with many a dark ravine, and studded with many a castle-like village and ruin. The broad summit of the range was a forest of hill-tops, separated here by a retired upland plain, there by a deep winding glen. On the east, the Jordan and its valley were hid behind the hills of Benjamin; but the chain of Moab and Gilead rose over them, a vast wall of azure built up against a golden sky, and streaked from base to summit with rich purple shadows. The mountain strongholds of Judah and Benjamin, renowned of yore in sacred story, or celebrated in sacred song, were all there grouped around me:—Gibeon, on its "hill;" Beth-horon, guarding the western pass; Beeroth and Beth-el: and away beyond them, rising from a troubled sea of hill-tops, "the rock Rimmon," where the six hundred, the shattered remnant of a guilty tribe, found an asylum;† Ramah of Benjamin, crowning its "height;" Gibeah of Saul, now a bare, desolate mount; Kirjath-jearim, perched on the side of "the hill," where the ark of the Lord remained for a time in the house of Abinadab;‡ Bethlehem, overlooking the wilderness; and Jerusalem, in the midst of all, seated in queenly state, begirt with mountains. That was a panorama

*Gen. xxviii. 14; Ps. cvii. 3.   †Judges xx. 45 48.   ‡1 Sam. vii. 1.

never be forgotten. Time cannot deface the picture. It remains photographed on my memory, calling up, as I look fondly back, many a stirring scene of Bible history and many a hallowed association.

Most probably this peak, from which the Western pilgrim has often got in days past, and often gets still, his first glance at the Holy City, was in Tasso's mind when he thus described the effect of "that first far view" upon the Crusaders:—

> "Lo, towered Jerusalem salutes the eyes!
> A thousand pointing fingers tell the tale;
> 'Jerusalem!' a thousand voices cry;
> 'All hail, Jerusalem!' hill, down, and dale
> Catch the glad sounds, and shout, 'Jerusalem, all hail!'"

It was here that Richard of England, having advanced from his camp at Ajalon, stood in sight of Jerusalem; but, burying his face in his mantle, he uttered the chivalrous exclamation: "O Lord God, I pray that I may never see thy Holy City, if I may not rescue it from the hands of thine enemies!"

A site so commanding as this could not have been overlooked in the early ages, when every hill had its city or fortress. There is much difference of opinion, however, as to its ancient name. A tradition as old as the sixth century makes it the Ramah, or Ramathaim-zophim, of the Old Testament—the birth-place, home, and burial-place of Samuel. A convent and church were subsequently erected on the spot in honour of the great prophet. The church is said to have been rebuilt by the Crusaders, who supposed this to be the ancient Shiloh. Now, within its shattered walls the Mohammedans have a mosque and a prayer-niche, and perform their devotions beside the traditional tomb of the Jewish prophet. Topography is decidedly against the tradition. There is no evidence to identify Neby Samwîl with Ramah.

But there can be little doubt that Neby Samwîl is the Mizpeh ("watch-tower") of Benjamin; the gathering-place of Israel, where the tribes assembled and bound themselves by an oath not to return to their homes till they had avenged on the inhabitants of Gibeah the rights of hospitality outraged by an abominable crime;* where they assembled afterwards, at the call of Samuel, to fight against the Philistines;† where they also assembled to elect their first king—and when Saul was chosen there was heard from this peak the loyal cry, "God save the king."‡ It would seem, too, that this is that very "high place of Gibeon" where Solomon offered a thousand burnt-offerings; and where the Lord, in answer to his prayer, gave him the wisdom that made him a world's proverb.§ It is therefore a spot of singular interest in connection with some of the most stirring and solemn incidents of Old Testament history.

---

*Judges xix. and xx.   †1 Sam. vii. 56.   ‡1 Sam. x. 24.   §1 Kings iii.

GIBEON.

AT the northern base of Mizpeh is a little upland plain, and in its centre is a low circular hill, with steep terraced sides and flat top. On the top stands the village of *Jîb,* the

EL-JÎB—GIBEON.

modern representative in name and site of the ancient capital of the wily Gibeonites. The name is descriptive, for *Gibeon* signifies "belonging to a *hill.*" We rode quickly down the steep from Neby Samwîl, across the intervening section of plain, and up the "hill" to the village. We were soon in the midst of the houses, examining the remains of an old castle and the massive fragments of ancient masonry which form the substructions of the modern dwellings. But the fountain—there is but one—was the main point of attraction. It is in a cave at the foot of a cliff. The cave seems to be artificial, excavated in the rock. Not far below it, among the olive-trees on the level ground, are the remains of a large open reservoir. This is doubtless that "pool of Gibeon," beside which Abner and Joab met at the head of the armies of Israel and Judah.

And there was enacted that bloody tragedy narrated in the Second Book of Samuel; and on the adjoining plain the rival generals met, and David's men gained a crowning victory.

But a still more famous battle was fought at an earlier period beneath the walls of Gibeon. Its old inhabitants, by a clever and romantic stratagem, had beguiled the Israelites into a league. Their Canaanite neighbours in consequence combined against them, and five Amorite kings attacked the Gibeonites. Messengers were sent to Joshua, then at Jericho, asking help. It was granted. In the evening he set out. All night his troops climbed the rugged defiles. In the early morning they crossed that rising ground on the east of the plain, and charged the Amorites, who fled in confusion. Now the narrative of the sacred writer becomes exceedingly graphic, and I read it with deepest interest on the spot. We rode on westward, to trace the line of flight and pursuit. The Israelites chased the enemy "along the way of the ascent of Beth-horon." A quarter of a mile west of Gibeon there is a sharp ascent to a ridge. Up this the Amorites fled, hard pressed by their pursuers. From the top of the ridge a long and rugged descent leads to Beth-horon, which is now seen in front, crowning a projecting shoulder of the hills. The nature of the ground here favoured the fugitives; but "as they fled from before Israel, while they were in the going down of Beth-horon, the Lord cast down great stones from heaven upon them unto Azekah, and they died." Joshua led the van of his troops. He saw that the victory was complete, but yet that approaching night must eventually save the Amorites from total destruction, by enabling a large body of them to escape in the darkness through the valley of Ajalon to their cities in the plain. Then it would seem that, standing on some commanding spot in sight of the Israelites, he uttered that wondrous prayer, glancing back towards Gibeon and forward upon Ajalon, "Sun, stand thou still upon Gibeon; and thou, Moon, in the valley of Ajalon."* Whatever opinion may be entertained by critics of the nature and effect of his wondrous prayer, the reader of the narrative on the spot cannot fail to be deeply impressed with the clearness and topographical accuracy of the description.

*Joshua x.

BETH-HORON.

THE poor Arab village, *Beit-'ûr el-Fôka*, "Beth-horon the Upper," has in itself nothing of importance. It stands on a little conical hill at the end of a rocky ridge, which extends from the western brow of the hills of Benjamin. The view from the terraced roof of the sheikh's house is wide and of no little interest, as it embraces the declivities and passes of Ephraim,

BEIT-'ÛR EL-FÔKA—UPPER BETH-HORON.

Benjamin, and Judah, with the plains of Sharon and Philistia. Some distance below the village is *Beth-horon the Nether*; and both those towns seem to have been in early times fortresses on one great road leading from Jerusalem to the Plain of Sharon. It was probably along this road St. Paul was conducted by Roman soldiers on his way to Cæsarea.

BEEROTH.

THE ride from Beth-horon to Beeroth, now called Bîreh, leads through one of the wildest regions of central Palestine. The road, where there is the trace of a road at all, is a mere goat-track, winding among rocks and stones, up and down rugged banks, across ravines, with

RUINED CHURCH AT EL-BÎREH—BEEROTH.

intervals of more open ground where there are little corn-fields and terraced vineyards and groves of olives. Bîreh is a large village situated on the crest of a ridge close to the great road from Jerusalem to Samaria and the north. There are in its houses large hewn stones, showing the antiquity of the site, It was one of the four cities of the Gibeonites in the time of Joshua; and from the many remains of ancient masonry among the modern houses and beside the fountain, it evidently continued to be a place of strength and importance to a late period of Jewish history. At present the only ruin worthy of note is a church of the Crusading age, built by the Templars, who owned the village during the reigns of the Latin kings of Jerusalem. It is said to have been erected on the spot where Mary and Joseph, on their return from Jerusalem with

Jesus, first discovered his absence from the company of their friends, and turned back in search of him. Whether there be any truth in the tradition or not, we are here on the road from Jerusalem to Nazareth, along which our Lord was taken then, and along which he often travelled afterwards.

BETH-EL.

BETH-EL, "the House of God," still retains in the modified Arab form, *Beitin*, its ancient holy name. It is the oldest sacred shrine in the country; but there is no trace of its pristine sacredness and glory there now. Beth-el has "come to nought." The modern poor hamlet

BEITIN—BETH-EL.

occupies the shelving point of a rocky ridge between two converging valleys. It is surrounded by higher ground on every side except the south; and yet its situation is so elevated that from some of the house-tops I saw the dome of the Great Mosque which stands on the site of the Temple of Jerusalem. Among the houses are remains of an old tower and of a Greek church. The spot, however, which specially attracted my attention was the little village fountain, and the great old reservoir, which it no doubt once filled with its tiny stream of water. A fountain cannot be obliterated or removed. It retains its position through all ages. It is, too, the invariable place of resort and rest for wayfarers. Beside it, doubtless, Abraham pitched his tent, and at it watered his flocks. Here Jacob rested and slept, as many a hardy Arab shepherd does still, with a stone for his pillow; here he dreamed of the ladder which reached from earth to heaven; and here he received those divine promises which cheered him through all the struggles and trials of his eventful life: "In thee and in thy seed shall all the families of the earth be blessed. And, behold, I am with thee, and will keep thee in all thy ways, in all places whither thou goest." He awoke, and cried with mingled joy and fear, "How dreadful is this place! this is none other than the House of God ! [BETH-EL]." Such was the origin of that name, revered during the whole of Jewish history, and still a household word throughout Christendom. It was a new baptism to the primeval village, for its Canaanitish name was *Luz,* as we are told in the Book of Genesis: "The name of the city was Luz at the first."* It is a singular fact that at a later period Beth-el and Luz are spoken of as if they were distinct places, for Joshua says of the common boundary of Ephraim and Benjamin that it ran "from Beth-el to Luz."† The explanation is probably this, that the earliest name of the *village* was Luz, and that Jacob gave the name Beth-el to the spot—doubtless beside the fountain—where he slept and saw the vision. Gradually the older name was displaced altogether by the new, so that village and place of prayer alike were called Beth-el. It is clear from the narrative in Genesis that the place where Jacob slept could not have been in the village, for we read that he "rose up early in the morning, and took the stone that he had put under his head, and set it up for a pillar, and poured oil upon the top of it. And he called the name of *that place* Beth-el, but the name of *the city* was Luz." There was no human witness to that solemn act of dedication. Jacob was alone with his God. The angels whom he had seen in the night vision "ascending and descending" on the ladder whose top reached to heaven, were witnesses of the consecration of both place and man to God's service.

To Beth-el Jacob returned after an interval of thirty years, during which the divine promise had been fulfilled so far as concerned his person and worldly prosperity. God had been with him, preserving him in all his goings, keeping him safe in the midst of dangers, and giving him a moral victory over his bitterest enemies. As we stand on that sacred spot, or look upon a picture of it, we may read with fresh interest the account of that second visit given by the sacred historian: "So Jacob came to Luz, which is in the land of Canaan (the same is Beth-el), he and all the people that were with him. And he built there an altar, and called the place EL-BETHEL [that is, The God of Beth-el] because there God was revealed unto him, when he fled from the face of his brother."‡ Here there is added this further record of grand promises, which concern not Jacob alone, nor his lineal descendants merely, but all mankind: "And God said unto him, Thy name is Jacob: thy name shall not be called any more Jacob, but Israel shall be thy name: and

*Gen. xxviii.   †Joshua xvi. 2.   ‡Gen. xxxv. 6.

he called his name Israel. And God said unto him, I am God Almighty: be fruitful and multiply; a nation and a company of nations shall be of thee, and kings shall come out of thy loins: and the land which I gave unto Abraham and Isaac, to thee I will give it, and to thy seed after thee will I give the land." And with this we connect the previous still more comprehensive promise: "I am the Lord, the God of Abraham thy father, and the God of Isaac…and thy seed shall be as the dust of the earth, and thou shalt spread abroad to the west, and to the east, and to the north, and to the south; and in thee and *in thy* SEED *shall all the families of the earth be blessed.*"* Standing there beside the fountain, I seemed, as I read the wondrous words, to look away back through the long vista of well-nigh four thousand years, and to behold the solitary patriarch bowed down in deep humility before God, and receiving with implicit faith and wondering joy, direct from Heaven, that grand blessing and promise. And I was led also to glance at history, that I might read there, inscribed in letters of light, the truth and fulfilment of God's sure word of prophecy and promise. From the pillar of a stone grew the sanctuary of Beth-el. The town became one of the national centres of assize and assembly in the time of Samuel.† At length, when it seemed on the point of being superseded by the new sanctuary at Jerusalem, it had attached to it a fresh, though evil celebrity, in being made one of the two holy places of the northern revolted kingdom.

Its subsequent history is a sad one. The town was assigned to Benjamin, but was captured by the Ephraimites. On the division of the kingdom of Israel it became doubly important, as a sanctuary, and as a border fortress, the key of both kingdoms. Jeroboam built a temple in it to rival Jerusalem. And here, on a great national festival, when Jeroboam stood in the temple beside the altar, a prophet from Judah suddenly advanced and pronounced divine judgment on an impious monarch and idolatrous rites: "O altar, altar, thus saith the Lord: Behold, a child shall be born unto the house of David, Josiah by name; and upon thee shall he sacrifice the priests of the high places that burn incense upon thee, and men's bones shall they burn upon thee. And he gave a sign the same day, saying, This is the sign which the Lord hath spoken: Behold, the altar shall be rent, and the ashes that are upon it shall be poured out. And it came to pass, when the king heard the saying of the man of God, which he cried against the altar in Beth-el, that Jeroboam put forth his hand from the altar, saying, Lay hold on him. And his hand, which he put forth against him, dried up, so that he could not draw it back again to him. The altar also was rent, and the ashes poured out from the altar, according to the sign which the man of God had given by the word of the Lord."‡ The sequel of the story is tragic yet instructive. The prophet of God, beguiled by a prophet of a different spirit, transgressed a divine command he had received, neither to eat nor drink in the sin-polluted city. The false prophet went after the man of God, when he had refused the king's invitation:

*Gen. xxviii. 13, 14.   †1 Sam. vii. 16.   ‡1 Kings xiii.

"And he said unto him, I also am a prophet as thou art; and an angel spake unto me by the word of the Lord, saying, Bring him back with thee into thine house, that he may eat bread and drink water. But he lied unto him." It was a base and cruel lie; and it proved fatal to the prophet of God: for, forgetful of the divine command, he turned back and ate and drank. Then he was warned by his unprincipled betrayer, who said to him, now by a true revelation from Heaven: "Thy carcase shall not come unto the sepulchre of thy fathers." And it was so; for, "when he was gone, a lion met him by the way, and slew him; and his carcase was cast in the way, and the ass stood by it; the lion also stood by the carcase." The lying prophet heard from his sons the fearful tale; and he went forth and laid the body of his victim in his own tomb.

Though the ancient sanctuary was thus cursed and polluted, its former glory attracted to it holy men. It became, in fact, a school of the prophets. The members of the school gathered round Elijah, when he passed through the town on the day he was taken up to heaven. It would appear that they were really taught of God there; for on that day they "came forth to Elisha, and said unto him, Knowest thou that the Lord will take away thy master from thy head to-day? And he said, Yea, I know it; hold ye your peace." But the people of Beth-el forgot their divine instructions. They renounced the God of their fathers—the God whom Jacob worshipped. The grievous sin of Jeroboam seems to have adhered to them; and the iniquity of the place in time became so glaring, so offensive, so polluting in its influences, that the name *Beth-el*, "House of God," was in the end changed by the prophet Hosea* into *Beth-aven*, "House of folly or idolatry." His words are very striking: "The inhabitants of Samaria shall be in terror for the calves of Beth-aven: for the people thereof shall mourn over it, and the priests thereof that rejoiced over it, for the glory thereof, because it is departed from it." One other incident in Beth-el's eventful history will be remembered here.† Josiah visited the city, and the "altar that was at Beth-el, and the high place which Jeroboam, the son of Nebat, who made Israel to sin, had made, even that altar and the high place he brake down: and he burned the high place and stamped it small to powder, and burned the grove [or image]. And as Josiah turned himself, he spied the sepulchres that were there in the mount; and he sent, and took the bones out of the sepulchres, and burned them upon the altar, and defiled it, according to the word of the Lord which the man of God proclaimed, who proclaimed these things. Then he said, What monument is that which I see? And the men of the city told him, It is the sepulchre of the man of God, which came from Judah, and proclaimed these things that thou hast done against the altar of Beth-el. And he said, Let him be; let no man move his bones. So they let his bones alone, with the bones of the prophet that came out of Samaria." No site in all Palestine is more suggestive of solemn and sacred incidents of Bible history than Beth-el.

*Hosea x. 5. †2 Kings xxiii. 15-18.

As I sat there at my tent door, near the little fountain, during the still evening of my visit, when the shadows were deepening in the glens, and the last rays of the declining sun were gilding the tops of rock and cliff, I read the story, and thought of its startling incidents and impressive lessons. Then I wandered forth and explored every part of the site. I tried to identify the spot where Jacob slept, and where he raised the stone pillow, and made it an altar, and called it the "House of God." I went to the rock sepulchres which were there in the cliffs around me, and whose dark openings dot the sides of the adjoining "mount," thinking that one or other of them was surely that of "the man of God from Judah," whose bones Josiah respected. Clambering, as darkness settled down, to the top of the shattered tower which crowns the hill of Beth-el, I looked long, and in sadness, over that dreary field of ruins, only tenanted now by a few poor shepherds; and I saw then, as I had never seen or felt before, how terribly time had fulfilled the prophetic doom: *"Beth-el shall come to nought."**

FROM BETH-EL TO AI, MICHMASH, ETC.

EARLY on the succeeding morning, with no little reluctance, I turned my back on Beth-el, and riding, without any path, across a rocky glen east of the ruins, I ascended to a hill-top in search of that place where Abraham pitched his tent and built his altar, as recorded in the Book of Genesis.† The exact spot is so definitely fixed and described that it is almost impossible to miss or mistake it: "And he removed from thence [Beth-el] unto the mountain on the east of Beth-el, and pitched his tent, having Beth-el on the west, and Ai on the east: and there he built an altar unto the Lord, and called upon the name of the Lord." Here I found a little plateau, stony but fertile, on the very crest of the hill; this, I thought, must have been the site of Abraham's camp and altar. It struck me forcibly, too, as I looked round on the vast panorama which suddenly opened before me to the eastward, that this must have been the exact scene of another incident of early Bible history which had a great effect on the future of the country, and which led indirectly to some remarkable events, physical, social, and national. From this plateau I commanded a view of the lower valley of the Jordan, and of a large portion of the Dead Sea, deep down at the foot of the dreary wilderness. One can here, in part at least, realize the fact that the Dead Sea lies in a profound chasm, its surface being thirteen hundred feet lower than the Mediterranean. Abraham went to Egypt for

*Amos v. 5. †Gen. xii. 8.

a time, to escape a famine in Palestine. On his return, he came with Lot to his favourite camping-ground on the east of Beth-el. Lot, his nephew, was with him; and their flocks and herds filled the whole country. It is probable that food and pasturage were more scanty than usual, owing to the recent famine and the drought which had occasioned it; and Abraham, we are told, "was very rich in cattle;" and Lot also, who went with him, "had flocks, and herds, and tents. And the land was not able to bear them, that they might dwell together; for their substance was great, so that they could not dwell together. And there was a strife between the herdmen of Abram's cattle and the herdmen of Lot's cattle." On seeing this, to avoid unseemly strife in the presence of strangers, Abraham proposed that they should separate; and with characteristic kindness and generosity he said, "Is not the whole land before thee? separate thyself, I pray thee, from me: if thou wilt take the left hand, then I will go to the right; or if thou wilt take the right hand, then I will go to the left." Lot does not appear to have shown an equal amount of self-denial. He saw the mountains around him parched and bare, and he "beheld all the plain of Jordan, that it was well watered everywhere.....like the garden of the Lord, like the land of Egypt," from which they had just come. Without a thought, apparently, of giving the choice to his uncle and benefactor, he chose "the plain of Jordan." It was a fatal choice, as the sequel proved; for though he had material prosperity for a short time, the gross immorality of the people among whom he chose to dwell corrupted his family and brought ruin and misery upon himself, his children, and his posterity. On that commanding height I read the Bible story with new interest. Every act and word of Abraham and Lot flashed before my mind with the vividness of reality; the herdmen wrangling on the hill-side; Abraham and Lot mediating and consulting—the one calm and conciliating, the other with longing, covetous eyes bent on the "well watered" plain of Jordan, not restrained by the proverbial wickedness of its people. And so they separated on this spot; and while Lot led his flocks down the declivities, "and moved his tent as far as Sodom," Abraham sought communion with God, who promised still more abundant blessings: "Lift up now thine eyes, and look from the place where thou art, northward and southward, and eastward and westward: for all the land which thou seest, to thee will I give it, and to thy seed for ever." I looked over that vast area when I read the words, and I could form some faint idea of the profound gratitude and astonishment of the patriarch. From the peaks around Hebron, away northward to the pale blue summits of Hermon and Lebanon; from the hill of Mizpeh on the west, across the Jordan eastward to the extreme limits of Moab and Gilead—all was promised. It was a grand inheritance. He could on the spot realize its extent. And then there followed to the aged man, who was as yet childless, the cheering words, "I will make thy seed as the dust of the earth." To an Eastern chief this is the choicest of all blessings. And it was soon realized in the birth of Isaac. The patriarch went away across that little plain by Luz, and southward along the mountain ridge to Mamre. While he rejoiced, doubtless, at such wondrous manifestations of divine favour, he mourned, too, over the waywardness and the worldliness of his nephew Lot.

When I stood on that hill-top, Beth-el was there behind me in full view on the west; but where was Ai, long-lost Ai ? On this, and on two other occasions since, I have explored the district in search of Ai. I believe I have been successful. Jutting out eastward from the little plateau on which I stood is a lower ridge, having deep glens on all sides, except where it joins the main chain. Spread over it I found traces of very ancient ruins, with cisterns, and caves, and rock-tombs, such as exist on the sites of all mountain cities in Palestine. At the eastern base are large quarries. I had no doubt then, after a careful examination of the whole site and ruins, and I have no doubt now, that here in ancient times stood Ai, "on the east" of Abraham's camp and altar. The site is suitable for an old Canaanite fortress, guarding the pass on the one side against the incursions of enemies from the Jordan valley; easily defended also from attacks of mountain-raiders on the west. The position agrees perfectly with the clear and specific incidental notices of the sacred historian; and reading the account of its capture by the Israelites while I sat amid the ruins, and saw the valleys that encompass it, and looked down the wild mountain pass to the plain of the Jordan far below, I was able to see how accurate and graphic is the narrative of Joshua.*

The capture of Ai forms one of the most romantic episodes in early Jewish history. It was a critical incident also in the conquest of Canaan. Failure would have been fatal. It would have disheartened the Israelites, and would have inspired the Canaanites with fresh courage and determination to resist the invaders of their country. The first assault was unsuccessful—the assailants were driven back in confusion, and with severe loss. This arose partly from over-confidence, but it was mainly intended to impress upon the people the inevitable consequences of national sin and guilt. When due expiation was made, by the punishment of Achan and his guilty house, another and successful attack was made. The judgment upon Achan was terrible; some have called it cruel and barbarous. But the whole circumstances must be taken into account. God himself was the leader of Israel. Achan's theft was a violation of God's covenant, an act of direct rebellion against the Almighty—a wilful act of disobedience and even contempt, prompted by the most sordid and selfish motives. To have passed it over with a light penalty would have tended to corrupt the whole nation, and to foster an entire disregard of the most express divine command. It was only under God's leadership the Israelites could ever expect to subdue the warlike people and capture the mountain-fortresses of Canaan. The strictest military discipline, and the most determined and severe repression and punishment of every form of mutiny, were, therefore, even from a human standpoint,

*Joshua vii. 2-5; viii. 1-29.

absolutely necessary. And it cannot be denied that it has always been extremely difficult to inspire in the Eastern mind those high principles of honesty, truth, and honour, which are, I am glad to say, to a large extent inherent in most of the Western peoples. To this day the inhabitants of Palestine, and Turkey generally, do not regard a lie or a dishonest act as disgraceful, especially if it happen to show great acuteness, and such tact as may make detection difficult or nearly impossible. At the time, too, when this most unfortunate and disgraceful theft was committed, the Israelites were exposed to unusual temptations. The wily Moabites, unable to resist the advance of Israel upon Palestine, tried to entice them to join in the gross and profligate rites of their national idolatry, as we read in the Book of Numbers; and they were to a considerable extent successful: "for they called the people [Israel] unto the sacrifices of their gods; and the people did eat, and bowed down to their gods. And Israel joined himself unto Baal-peor"*—most licentious and corrupt even among the deities of Canaan. In the plain of Jericho, also, where they were now encamped, they had all round them a people of hereditary immorality. Such reflections one can scarcely exclude from his mind as he stands upon the heights of Ai and reads the romantic story of its capture.†

The second assault on the city was skilfully planned, and had, besides, the direct sanction of the God of battles. To the north-west of Ai, between it and Beth-el, is a little rocky glen, across which I rode on my way from the latter village. In it, during the night preceding the final attack, five thousand chosen Israelites were placed in ambush. Joshua and the main body took up a position on the high ridge north of Ai, but separated from it by a deep glen. This was also effected during the night, unknown to the besieged. Having made all his arrangements with the skill of an experienced general, Joshua went down into the valley in front of the fortress; and in the morning, before it was yet light, he led his troops forward, as if about to make a direct attack up the steep from the east. The first dawn revealed him to the watchful foe, who immediately leaving Ai in force, charged impetuously down the hill. "And Joshua and all Israel made as if they were beaten before them, and fled by the way of the wilderness"—down the wild defiles toward the plain. The stratagem was perfectly successful. "All the people that were in the city were called together to pursue after them: and they pursued after Joshua, and were drawn away from the city. And there was not a man left in Ai or Beth-el, that went not out after Israel: and they left the city open...And the Lord said unto Joshua, Stretch out the javelin [or spear] that is in thine hand toward Ai." It appears to have been a preconcerted signal as well as a divine command, for God was leader of his host. "And the ambush arose quickly out of their place, and they ran as soon as he had stretched out his hand, and entered into the city, and took it; and they hasted and set the city on fire. And when the men of Ai looked behind them, they saw,

*Num. xxv. 2, 3. †Joshua viii. 1-29.

and, behold, the smoke of the city ascended up to heaven, and they had no power to flee this way or that way: and the people that fled to the wilderness turned back upon their pursuers." They were completely paralyzed. There was no safety, no help for them now. All were put to the sword, and Ai was razed to the ground. "So Joshua burnt Ai, and made it an heap for ever, even a desolation unto this day"—the day when the historian wrote. Some centuries later Ai appears to have been in part rebuilt; but it is now, and has been for a thousand years or more, a desolate ruin.

Should any of my readers ever visit this site, I recommend him to read the narrative there, as I did. I was deeply impressed on the site of Ai, as I have often been when travelling elsewhere through Bible lands, with the graphic descriptions of the sacred writers, and the minuteness of their topographical details. Not only as regards natural scenery, but also as regards Eastern character, and costume, and habits, and mode of warfare, the sacred penmen show an intimate acquaintance with the subjects on which they write. Often, in a sentence or two, a picture is drawn which has the accuracy of a photograph, not unfrequently combined with the bright colouring of a landscape by Claude, or the life-like and strongly-marked features of a portrait by Rembrandt. One can almost fancy he sees a David in every mountain shepherd he meets among the rocks of the wild goats in the wilderness of Judah, or here amid the passes of Benjamin. And should he cross the Jordan to yonder hills of Gilead and Moab, every village chief or Arab sheikh he meets might serve as a study for a portrait of Elijah, or Joshua, or Esau. The features of the country remain unchanged. We see them now as they were seen by Abraham and Lot, and by Joshua and the invading hosts of Israel, the bare and rugged mountains, and the rich and well-watered plain of the Jordan. The inhabitants, too, have not changed in character. The mountaineers are as fierce as of yore. And as to the people of Jericho, and the plain of Sodom around it, the fertile soil and enervating climate produced in early ages an effeminate, corrupt, and sensual race, whose shameless profligacy made the name of their chief city a term of infamy; and strange to say, the few inhabitants who still dwell in the mud hovels of Jericho, or pitch their ragged tents upon its plain, are notorious for the worst vices of their forefathers.

Looking northward from the heights of Ai, we see, about two miles distant, a conical white hill with a large village near its base. It is the *Rock Rimmon*, on which the six hundred Benjamites took refuge from the just wrath of their brethren. There they lived for four months, till at length the Israelites "repented for Benjamin their brother." The story of the abominable crime of a portion of the tribe, and the terrible retribution of the outraged nation, is recalled even by a distant view of the Rock.

MICHMASH.

FROM Ai I rode down the rocky ravine through which the Israelites had fled from their enemies; and then, climbing the south bank of the glen, I passed over bare undulating table-land to the hamlet of *Mŭkhmâs*, the modern representative of the ancient Michmash, one of the strongholds of Benjamin. There are foundations of large stones in and around the houses, and broken columns may be noticed here and there, showing the former strength and importance of the place. It stands on a prominent ridge, shelving down to the eastward, and having on the south the deep ravine of Wady es Suweinît. On the opposite ridge, beyond the valley, is the little village of *Jebâ*, the Geba of Benjamin.

The principal object I had in view when I first visited the bleak and rugged region was to inspect the scene of Jonathan's romantic and successful adventure against the Philistines. The two strongholds of Michmash and Geba stood facing and in full view of each other, scarcely a mile apart, on opposite sides of the ravine. The ravine near the villages has steep banks, broken here and there with rocks and crags, but passable for active footmen, and even for horses. But half a mile farther down, the ravine contracts into a narrow gorge, with lofty naked cliffs on each side. Above the cliff on the Michmash side are a few acres of level table-land.

WADY ES SUWEINÎT, NEAR MŬKHMÂS.
(*Scene of Jonathan's Exploit.*)

Riding down to this spot, and examining the features of the ravine, the cliffs, and the ridges above them, I felt convinced that this was the scene of Jonathan's wild exploit.

The Philistines had held Geba for a time, but Jonathan drove them out and occupied the place. The Philistines, hearing of this defeat, assembled in great force, and "pitched in Michmash." The Israelites fled on all sides, some to the Jordan valley, others across the Jordan to Gad and Gilead. Saul was at Gilgal, near Jericho. Samuel at length arrived, and infused some spirit into the fainting hearts of Saul's few followers—only numbering six hundred. "And Saul and Jonathan, and the people that were present with them, abode in Geba of Benjamin;" that village on the top of the ridge south of the ravine. "The Philistines encamped in Michmash;" and resolving to force the pass, they left the town and advanced to the edge of the ravine. One company, we read, "turned the way of the border that looketh down upon the valley of Zeboim [Suweinît] toward the wilderness." They took up a position on that piece of table-land over the narrowest part of the ravine. The Israelites, few in number and dispirited by long oppression, retreated over the hills to Migron, near Gibeah of Saul. Jonathan now seeing the harassed state of his country, and the despair both of his father and of his followers, resolved to make a bold attempt to surprise the enemy's camp. The cause of his sudden resolve and his hope of success he thus explained to his armour-bearer: "Come and let us go over unto the garrison of these uncircumcised; it may be that the Lord will work for us; for there is no restraint to the Lord to save by many or by few." His armour-bearer appears to have had much of his own spirit of faith and courage, and he replied: "Do all that is in thine heart: turn thee, behold I am with thee according to thy heart." The nature of the ground favoured the bold enterprise. "Between the passes by which Jonathan sought to go over unto the Philistines' garrison, there was a rocky crag on the one side, and a rocky crag on the other side…The one crag rose up on the north in front of Michmash, and the other on the south in front of Geba." Jonathan said, "We will pass over unto the men, and we will discover ourselves unto them." Stealthily and cautiously, as well-trained mountaineers, they descended the southern cliff, screened from view by projecting rocks. Then they climbed the northern crag to a place where, by stepping out on a projecting ledge, they would be in sight of the Philistines, and yet far enough off to effect their escape if necessary. Advancing from behind a rock, they suddenly showed themselves to the enemy, who were naturally astonished on seeing them so close to the camp, and they said to each other, "Behold, the Hebrews come forth out of the holes where they have hid themselves." They could not otherwise account for such a singular visit. Jonathan had, in the true spirit of his direct dependence on God, given his companion a testing sign to show whether God would indeed favour their attempt. "If they say thus unto us, Tarry until we come to you; then we will stand still in our place, and will not go up unto them. But if they say thus, Come up unto up; then we will go up: for the Lord hath delivered them into our hand; and this shall be the sign unto us." The sign was favourable. The moment the Philistines saw them they said: "Come up to us... And Jonathan climbed up upon his hands and upon his feet, and his armour-bearer after him; and they fell before Jonathan; and his armour-bearer slew after him." A sudden panic seized the whole host. The Lord fought for Israel. The strange and unexpected onslaught, and the simultaneous shock of an earthquake, created such terror and confusion that the Philistines fought with each other. "There was a trembling in the camp, in the field, and among the people: the garrison, and the spoilers, they also trembled, and the earth quaked: so that there was an exceeding great trembling."*

From the heights of Geba, on the other side of the ravine, Saul's watchmen saw the Philistine army melting away, and running distractedly "hither and thither." Saul's ear soon caught the din of battle. Collecting his men with all speed, he crossed the pass and joined in the slaughter and pursuit. Swiftly the tidings sped over hill and dale, through city and village. The new and joyful words were in every mouth, "The Philistines flee;" and with speed the men of Israel rush forth from cave, and rock, and stronghold, and join in pursuit of the hated foe. The battle of Michmash was the first of those fierce conflicts carried on at intervals throughout the protracted reigns of Saul and David, and which eventually resulted in the expulsion of the Philistines from the mountains of Israel.

This sketch of the romantic adventure of Jonathan is another and most striking illustration of the wonderful correspondence of the descriptions of events in Bible history with the places where they were enacted in Bible lands. Every detail of the stirring adventure, as recorded in the First Book of Samuel, I have here followed on the old stage. The graphic story became a life scene as I read it on the banks of the ravine. I saw Geba and Michmash up there on opposite sides; I saw the sharp projecting twin cliffs; I saw the tableland where the Philistines temporarily halted; I saw the clefts, and rugged rocks, and deep ravines, and mountain caves in the country around me, where the terror-stricken Israelites could so easily hide themselves, and from which, when the danger passed, they could so easily issue forth, and join in pursuit of fleeing oppressors. It was a scene of surpassing interest to a Bible student and to a Christian pilgrim in Palestine. I should wish to conduct my reader to the spot; but I can only place before him a faithful picture of the ravine and the cliffs.

Another point I must not omit. The modern inhabitants of Michmash seem to inherit much of the fierce and predatory spirit of their predecessors, both Canaanites and Philistines. They dogged me wherever I went, muttering curses and threats deep and stern, at first asking and in the end demanding *bakshish*. I took no notice of them further than was absolutely necessary for my purpose of minute examination. When, at length, having finished my survey of the battle-field and a rough sketch of the pass, I

*1 Sam. xiii. 16-18; xiv. 1-16.

mounted my horse to ride to Geba, they drew up before me in formidable array, and swore by the life of the Prophet I should not move. I insisted, however, in breaking through their ranks; and fortunately for me their valour did not go beyond presenting two or three old matchlocks at my head, and, with tremendous noise and fury, brandishing swords and daggers. The goat-track by which I had to descend into the glen was, perhaps, quite as dangerous to life and limb as the arms of the lawless vagabonds of Michmash. I have been on many bad roads in my Syrian wanderings,—I have ridden my Arab horse to the very highest peaks of Hermon and Lebanon,—but the Pass of Michmash is the worst I ever encountered.

Geba is not to be confounded with *Gibeah*, the birth-place of Saul. Both were fortified towns of the Canaanites, and both were allotted to Benjamin. Geba retains its ancient name in the modern form Jeba. It is now a very small and poor village. There is, however, in it a square tower of great solidity and apparent antiquity, also a little building like a church. The situation is commanding, as it overlooks the bleak declivities and ravines down to the Jordan valley. The bright green fringe that marks the tortuous course of the river through its broad and now desolate plain is very distinctly seen, and one would suppose it was only three or four miles distant, while in reality it is nearly twenty. The inhabitants of Geba are like their neighbours of Mishmash, at least I found them so in both my visits—notorious robbers. They are ready to take advantage of every unprotected wayfarer. They do not seem even to have the good quality of courage and open daring like the wandering Arabs. They are cunning, treacherous, and cowardly. They rarely venture upon a direct attack on any one; but they will throw stones, and even fire a shot from a safe distance. On one occasion I had a narrow escape when making a sketch in the ravine of Suweinît. I had left my horse at some little distance with my servant, and had taken a seat on a projecting ledge. I was startled ere long by a sharp report from the opposite side of the ravine, and a bullet struck the cliff within a few yards of me. Fortunately they are not good marksmen those bandits of Geba, and their rifles are not of the first quality.

This whole region, from the top of the ridge at Jerusalem, Bethel, Bethlehem, and as far south as Hebron, down to the Jordan valley and the Dead Sea, might be justly described in general terms as a "den of thieves." It is quite as dangerous now to go from Jerusalem to Jericho as it was in the days of our Lord; and the very same fatality would be most likely to happen to any unwary and unprotected traveller now as happened to the man in the parable of the Good Samaritan. I have had some experience of the fact. When on my way to the east of the Jordan, with a pretty strong Arab escort, a few years ago, I found it necessary to engage at Jerusalem, as far as Jericho, the agent or sheikh, of the robber tribes that infest the wilderness of Judea. He acts, strange to say, under the authority of the Turkish pasha of Jerusalem, and levies a certain amount of black-mail upon all travellers who pass this way. He was, as I saw him, a fine specimen of the bandit chief, splendidly mounted, and armed with rifle, revolvers, and scimitar. We considered it unquestionably safer to follow such a personage than unexpectedly to meet him in some ravine between Jerusalem and Jericho. All went well; but we saw quite enough to show us the prudence of our consul's advice in engaging as escort the sheikh of Abu Dis—such is the name of his village. Just at the top of the last long descent into the Jordan valley the road runs for a few hundred yards along the edge of Wady el-Kelt, the "brook Cherith" of Scripture, where Elijah found a hiding-place from Ahab, and where "the ravens brought him bread and flesh" morning and evening.* It is a wild and withal a dangerous spot. On the left is the ravine, a thousand feet deep, like a rent in the mountain-side, with a torrent forcing its way, in a line of white foam, between the cliffs at the bottom. We halted for a moment on the narrow ledge of rock along which our path lay, to look down into the ravine and out between the cliffs upon the plain of Jericho, now opening before us. Suddenly I heard a wild shout overhead, and raising my eyes I saw a band of Arabs, numbering perhaps twenty or thirty, ranged along the crest of rocks that line and command the narrow path. We did not know what might be their intentions; for, as they squatted there, glaring at us, they fingered their long matchlocks with nervous eagerness. We were completely in their power. I have seldom seen such a hungry-looking set of savages. Their arms, legs, and breasts were bare; their hair streamed down in tangled plaits, scarcely confined by the dirty rags that served for *kufiyehs*; and the scanty brown shirts, which formed their whole clothing, were all in tatters. Our Adwân escort from the east of the Jordan positively seemed gentlemen in contrast with those robbers of the wilderness of Judea. Those are the scoundrels that infest this road, and indeed the greater part of this region. I called to their chief, who had fallen behind. He rode up, waved his hand, and, much to our relief, the whole gang disappeared in a moment. We saw no more of them. Had their chief not been with us our passage would have been dangerous, if not impossible. A few days later we met a Damascus merchant, who had foolishly attempted to come down from Jerusalem without the recognized guardian. He was seized, robbed, stripped naked, and wounded. He would probably have died had he not, fortunately, fallen in with a party of travellers who acted the part of the good Samaritan.

We return to Geba. Standing there all alone on that bare, sun-scorched ridge, looking down over barren hills and white rocks upon the great valley of the Jordan, Geba seems the very type of desolation. The curse has fallen heavily upon "Geba of Benjamin." When Elisha came up the defile we see below us, from Jericho to Beth-el, forests clothed the surrounding hills;† now there is not a tree—there is scarcely a green shrub—in the whole landscape. Vineyards then covered the terraced sides of glen and hill from

*1 Kings xvii. 1-7.   †2 Kings ii. 24.

base to summit. Traces of the terraces are still there, but the vines have disappeared. Cities and fortresses, in the days of Israel's power, crowned every peak and studded every ridge above where we stood at Geba; shapeless mounds of ruin and rubbish now mark their deserted sites. From the little tower of Geba no less than nine ruined towns and villages were pointed out to me. I could not fail to call to mind here, as I did on many another spot in Palestine, the striking prophetic judgments pronounced by Moses long, long centuries ago. He foresaw the sins of the people ere they had yet entered the Promised Land;—he foresaw their rebellion against that gracious Lord who had led them, and fed them in the desert; he foresaw their base ingratitude, their idolatry, their gross immorality, their blasphemies. He solemnly warned them of their danger, and then he wrote these terrible words, the fulfilment of which we now see at every stage of our pilgrimage journey: "If ye will not for all this hearken unto me, but walk contrary unto me; then I will walk contrary unto you in fury; and I will also chastise you seven times for your sins…And I will destroy your high places…And I will make your cities waste, and will bring your sanctuaries into desolation…And I will bring the land into desolation and your enemies which dwell therein shall be astonished at it. And you will I scatter among the nations, and I will draw out the sword after you: and your land shall be a desolation."* The words of the prophetic curse are terrible; and the state of the country, as we now see it in passing through, is no less terrible.

Another striking portion of the Old Testament can be studied with advantage in travelling along the route we are now following. It is the graphic description of the Assyrian advance upon Jerusalem given in the tenth chapter of Isaiah. Every stage of the army's progress is so clearly laid down that we can follow it. The general with his troops turns aside, as it would seem, from the great northern road near Beth-el, and moves eastward to Aiath; that is, Ai. Then he passes through Migron, a place not yet identified. Michmash is the next stage; and there he lays up his baggage, unable at the moment to convey it across the deep ravine. The narrative thus proceeds: "They are gone over the pass [the men without baggage]; they have taken up their lodging at Geba; Ramah trembleth." Ramah (now Er-Ram) is situated half an hour to the west of Geba. Then the prophet adds: "Gibeah of Saul is fled;"—it stood on the top of a conspicuous hill, visible from Geba, and when the dreaded foe came in sight its people fled. In the morning the army continues its march. The sites of Gallim and Laish are unknown; they were doubtless small villages not far distant from Gibeah. Anathoth is in the direct line of march—"O thou poor Anathoth." The evening finds them at Nob, within sight of Jerusalem— "This very day shall he halt at Nob: he shaketh his hand at the mount of the daughter of Zion, the hill of Jerusalem."

The writer evidently knew and marked each step on the line of march of the invading

*Lev. xxvi. 27-33.

army. Like a true and accurate historian, he studied closely the topography of the country, and he has left us a narrative such as a modern military engineer might have written. The more closely I study my Bible, the more carefully I compare it with the country where it was penned, the more convinced do I become of its perfect truthfulness and its divine authority.

ANATHOTH.

ANATHOTH is barely three miles south of Geba, yet the road is so bad, the intervening glens are so deep and rugged, that I was a full hour in reaching it. Were it not for its sacred associations no man would dream of visiting Anathoth. Anâta is the modern name; and it is a poor hamlet of some twenty houses, standing on a broad, dreary ridge, among gray rocks and gray ruins. There are a few fields around it, dotted at long intervals with a half-withered fig or olive tree, as if a curse lay upon it. There are portions of a wall, built of ancient masonry; and there are a few fragments of columns lying about in the dust, telling a sad story of departed grandeur. There is no verdure, no beauty, no richness, scarcely a sign of life. Yet Anathoth, in the land of Benjamin, was one of the cities allotted to the Levites more than three thousand years ago. And it has even a prouder title to distinction: it was the birthplace of the prophet Jeremiah.* Here he received his first commission to warn and threaten a rebellious nation;† and here, amid mountain solitudes and rocky dells, he mourned and wept at the foreseen calamities of his beloved country. When I looked over that

"Barren desert, fountainless and dry,"

of which Anathoth commands a prospect wide and wild, his words seemed filled with a double power and pathos: "Oh that my head were waters, and mine eyes a fountain of tears, that I might weep day and night for the slain of the daughter of my people! Oh that I had in the wilderness a lodging place of wayfaring men; that I might leave my people, and go from them!"‡ One can trace, in nearly all the images and illustrations with which Jeremiah's writings abound, the influence of those wild scenes amid which he passed his boyhood, and which were before him on every visit to his early home. Mountains, rocks, wild beasts, shepherds, are again and again introduced; and when predicting the utter ruin of Israel he says, with a characteristic allusion to the peculiar position of Anathoth: "Spoilers are come upon all the bare heights in the wilderness; for the sword

*Jer. i. 1. †Jer. i. 5, 19. ‡Jer. ix. 1, 2.

devoureth from the one end of the land even to the other end of the land: no flesh hath peace.* The view from Anathoth is dreary, and painfully desolate; the people are rude as their country; and yet a visit to the site of the old city is singularly instructive to the thoughtful student of the Book of Jeremiah.

GIBEAH OF SAUL.

LOOKING westward from Anathoth, my eye caught, at the distance of about a mile, the white top of a conical hill rising over an intervening ridge. "What is the name of that tell?" I said to an old shepherd at my side. "Tuleil el-Fûl," he replied. Seven long hours I had been in the saddle, under a cloudless sun, in a most inhospitable land. I had not enjoyed, even for a moment, "the shadow of a great rock" in that waste, weary country; yet the surpassing, all-absorbing interest of holy sites and holy associations, made me for the time insensible to fatigue. Tuleil el-Fûl, I knew, was covered of yore with the buildings of Gibeah, the city which, by its abominable crime, brought such calamities upon the whole tribe of Benjamin; the city, too, which gave Israel its first king; and which witnessed the unparalleled tenderness and devotion of poor bereaved Rizpah.†

I could not resist the longing to visit it, and half an hour's hard riding brought me to its base. Several times since I have stood upon its summit, and wandered round it, endeavouring to fix the exact sites of incidents connected with the history of Saul, and of David and Jonathan. A rude cairn on the hill-top, a few massive foundations now supporting terraces on the hill-side, and some scattered ruins at its western base, alone mark the site of the ancient royal city of Benjamin. Its very name has gone, unless indeed the Arabic *Tuleil* ("little hill") be a translation of the Hebrew *Gibeah*.

Gibeah was the scene of Saul's mad freaks, of David's musical powers in soothing his evil spirit, and of Jonathan's devoted friendship. Here, also, took place one of the most terrible acts of retributive justice on record.‡ Saul, in his madness and cruelty, had persecuted, and even attempted to exterminate, the Gibeonites, whom Joshua had solemnly sworn to protect. The punishment for this act of treachery on the part of Saul was a three years' famine in the reign of David. The Lord's answer to David's earnest pleading for mercy was, "It is for Saul, and for his bloody house, because he put to death the Gibeonites." In order to vindicate the divine law, seven of Saul's sons were delivered up to the Gibeonites, "and they hanged them in the mountain before the Lord, and they fell

*Jer. xii. 12.   †2 Sam. xxi. 8.   ‡2 Sam. xxi. 1-10.

all seven together: and they were put to death in the days of harvest, in the first days, at the beginning of barley harvest." Two of the victims were sons of Rizpah, one of Saul's wives. And then followed an act of unparalleled maternal devotion: "And Rizpah took sackcloth, and spread it for her upon the rock, from the beginning of harvest until water was poured upon them from heaven; and she suffered neither the birds of the air to rest on them by day, nor the beasts of the field by night." Standing by that hill, and looking up at the bare rock on its side where the bodies were left exposed, one cannot fail to recall the wondrous endurance of the poor mother, watching under a scorching sun by day, and in biting cold by night, for at least four long months, with the wasting skeletons of her sons ever before her eyes.

From Gibeah there is a wide and most interesting view, embracing the uplands of Benjamin and Judah, extending northward to Beth-el, and southward to the heights beyond Bethlehem. It was in all respects suitable for the residence and central government of the first king of Israel.

NOB.

RIDING from Gibeah to Jerusalem, my attention was attracted by a conspicuous conical hill near the road, and about half a mile south of Gibeah. I found on its sides and top traces of a small but very ancient town—cisterns hewn in the rock, large building stones, portions of the hill cut away and levelled, and the ruins of an old tower. From it I got a clear though distant view of Mount Zion; Moriah and Olivet being hid by an intervening ridge. It is the first point, I believe, on the northern road from which Mount Zion can be seen. I felt convinced at the time, and subsequent examination served to deepen the conviction, that this is the site of the long-lost *Nob*. And I here saw how very graphic, from beginning to end, was the description of the march of the Assyrian host upon Jerusalem, to which I have already referred in my remarks on Geba. I had followed the line of march from Ai to Michmash, and from Michmash to Geba; and now, standing on the top of this hill, I understood the full meaning of the prophet's last sentence: "This very day shall he halt at Nob: he shaketh his hand at the mount of the daughter of Zion, the hill of Jerusalem."

Between Gibeah and Nob is a deep retired vale, which was most probably the scene of the affecting interview between David and Jonathan.* David seeing that his life was in imminent danger at Saul's court in Gibeah, went to Nob, then a noted sanctuary, and

---

*1 Sam. xx.

the residence of the high priest. Jonathan had tried to propitiate his father on behalf of David, but in vain. There was nothing to save David from the tyrant's rage except flight. Going to Abimelech, the high priest at Nob, he got Goliath's sword, and escaped to the Philistines at Gath. But that brief visit of David sealed the fate both of Abimelech and Nob. A base Edomite betrayed the innocent priest; and when no Israelite dared to carry out the cruel orders of the tyrant king, Doeg proved a willing executioner. Abimelech and his whole family were murdered: "And Doeg the Edomite turned, and he fell upon the priests, and he slew on that day fourscore and five persons that did wear a linen ephod. And Nob, the city of the priests, smote he with the edge of the sword, both men and women, children and sucklings, and oxen and asses and sheep." It was an act of savage cruelty, for which the vengeance of Heaven came upon the guilty king and his "bloody house." Sitting on the hill, amid the ruins, I read the horrid story; and I could not help shuddering as I saw the rocks, once stained with the blood of the innocent victims. Can we wonder that Ezekiel* was commissioned to pronounce a curse upon Palestine, when he could with so much truth assign as its cause, "The land is full of bloody crimes"?

We return to Jerusalem, "The City of the Great King," where miracles of divine love and mercy may serve to obliterate harrowing memories of war and bloodshed. Here upon the side of Olivet, looking down on Gethsemane and across the Kidron to Calvary, I bid my readers farewell.

*Ezek. vii. 22.

APPENDIX.

THE SITE OF CALVARY.

IT may be interesting to my readers to have before them the several views hitherto set forth regarding the true site of Calvary.

1. The *traditional site* is within the Church of the Sepulchre. The approach to it is by a flight of steps from the south transept. Going up, we enter a vaulted chamber, now named the *Chapel of the Elevation of the Cross*. It is about fourteen feet higher than the floor of the church. At its eastern end is a platform ten feet long and eighteen inches high. In the centre stands the altar, richly decorated. Under the altar is a hole in the marble slab, communicating with a similar one in the natural rock below. In this hole, it is said, the cross of our Lord was fixed. Near it, on the right, is an opening in the marble revealing the rent in the rock occasioned by the earthquake, as recorded by St. Matthew (xxvii. 51). The holes for the crosses of the two malefactors are shown to the right and left, at the ends of the altar, about five feet distant from that in the centre. Adjoining this chapel, on the south, is the *Chapel of the Crucifixion* so called because it stands on or over the spot where our Lord was nailed to the cross. Under the *Chapel of the Elevation of the Cross* is a low crypt-like chamber, called the *Chapel of Adam*.

These traditions can be traced back as far as the fourth century, when the Bordeaux pilgrim indicated the spot. Eusebius informs us that the Emperor Constantine removed an accumulation of earth and rubbish from the Holy Sepulchre and Golgotha, and built a church over them. The story of Eusebius is repeated by subsequent writers. Jerome mentions a tradition to the effect that Adam was buried in Golgotha, and that this name was given to the place because the skull of Adam was there preserved. A later tradition affirms that the blood of Christ flowed down through the rent rock, and falling upon the head of Adam restored him to life.

The first to call in question the authenticity of the traditional site was Korte, a German, in 1738. He was followed by Clarke, Robinson, Tobler, and others; while Kraft, Williams, and many others, affirm the truth of the tradition.

2. The most recent view is that adopted by Captain Conder, Dr. Merill, General Gordon, and others. In 1878 Captain Conder, in his "Tent Work in Palestine," stated his conviction that the real site of Calvary was to be found on a rocky knoll outside the northern wall and close to the cave known as "Jeremiah's Grotto." It is just "without the gate" now called the Damascus Gate, and is a rocky precipice of about fifty feet high, at a distance of five hundred feet from the city wall. The top of the knoll is rounded and dome-like, and is one hundred and ten feet higher than the Sacred Rock of the Temple, of whose enclosure it commands a view. "A sort of amphitheatre is formed by the gentle slopes on the west; and the whole population of the city might easily witness from the vicinity anything taking place on the top of the cliff. The knoll is just beside the main north road. It is occupied by a cemetery of Muslim tombs, which existed as early as the fifteenth century at least…The hill is quite bare, with scanty grass covering the rocky soil, and a few irises and wild flowers growing among the graves. Not a tree or shrub exists on it, though fine olive groves stretch northward from its vicinity…The hillock is rounded on all sides but the south, where the yellow cliff is pierced by two small caves high up in the sides…In 1881 it was found that a Jewish tomb existed on a smaller knoll west of the north road, about two hundred yards from the top of the first-mentioned knoll" ("Survey of Western Palestine," Jerusalem volume, p. 432). Of this tomb Captain Conder writes: "The whole is very rudely cut in the rock, which is of inferior quality. The doorway is much broken, and there is a loophole or window, four feet wide, on either side of the door. The outer court, cut in the rock, is seven feet square; and two stones are so placed in this as to give the idea that they may have held in place a rolling-stone before the door. On the right is a side entrance, leading into a chamber with a single *loculus*. The chamber within the tomb entrance is reached by a descent of two steps, and measures six feet by nine feet. From either side wall and from the back wall is an entrance leading into a side chamber. A passage runs in continuation of each entrance, and on each side is a bench about two and a half feet wide by two and a quarter high."

Captain Conder continues, after stating his view that the adjoining mound was the place of public execution: "It would be bold to hazard the suggestion that the single Jewish sepulchre thus found is indeed the tomb in the garden, nigh unto the place called Golgotha; yet its appearance so near the old place of execution and so far from other tombs in the old cemeteries of the city is extremely remarkable."

A Jewish tradition points to this hill as the "Beth-has-sekîlah," or "house of stoning;" while early Christian tradition fixes it as the scene of the martyrdom of Stephen. According to Dr. Chaplin, the Jews to this day designate the knoll as the "place of stoning." The hill, in certain lights, appears to present a striking resemblance to a human skull. The adoption of this site by Dr. Chaplin, Dr. Merill, and by the late General Gordon, has helped to give it considerable popularity.

3. Dr. Barclay, author of "The City of the Great King," who spent many years in Jerusalem, writes as follows: "That the idea of 'a skull' is some way or other involved in the Hebrew" and Greek names is evident; "but whether because skull-shaped, or a place bestrewed with skulls, admits of some doubt. The probabilities are rather in favour of the former...Now, there is a kind of head or promontory projecting into the Kidron Valley, a short distance above Gethsemane, to which such a term seems quite applicable...May not this be the site of that awful scene—the crucifixion of the Son of God?...The garden and sepulchre were no doubt on the lower side of the road, perhaps quite down in the gloomy vale of the Kidron. There are still some old sepulchres to be found there, answering quite well the description of the Redeemer's sepulchre."

This view accords with that I was led to adopt when in Jerusalem, previous to the visit of Dr. Barclay.

4. The *true site* of Calvary, the place where our Lord was crucified, is, as indicated in the text, page 72, unknown. The name *Calvary* is the Latin rendering of the Hebrew *Golgotha* and the Greek *Cranion*, "a skull." The only statements given by New Testament writers as to its position are, that it was "without the gate," "nigh to the city." St. John says that after the scene in the Judgment Hall of Pilate, in the fortress of Antonia, "they took Jesus; and he went forth bearing the cross, unto the place called the place of a skull, which is called in Hebrew Golgotha." It was apparently a well-known place, bearing both a Greek and Hebrew name, and outside the gate, not far from Antonia. From the account in the Gospel of St. Matthew, it would seem as if it was close to a public road, where there were passers-by, and as if it could be clearly seen from a distance; for he says, "And many women were there beholding from afar." Another statement in St. John's Gospel is interesting: "Now in the place where he was crucified there was a garden; and in the garden a new tomb...There they laid Jesus."

Guided by these several passages, I carefully and repeatedly examined the city and its environs, and I was led to the conclusion that Calvary was outside St. Stephen's Gate, which is close to the citadel of Antonia; and that it was on the high ground a little northward, on the brow of the Kidron, within full view from the side of the Mount of Olives, where the women could with safety behold "from afar;" beside it also runs a public road, northward, and another over Kidron, eastward. Here in the side of the Kidron are a number of tombs hewn in the rock; and there was probably a terraced garden here also in former days, as there are such gardens now along the banks of the valley. It seemed to me that this spot corresponded more fully than any other to the accounts given by the sacred writers of "the place called the place of a skull, which is called in Hebrew Golgotha," where Jesus was crucified, and where there was a garden, and "in the garden a new tomb," in which "they laid him."

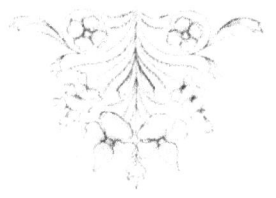

INDEX.

ABASSIDES, 55.
Abd-el-Melek, 48.
Abraham, 9, 22, 31, 48, 80.
Abraham and Lot, 151.
Absalom's Tomb, 18, 31, 80, 88, 89.
Abu-Ghaush, xx.
Abu Nabut, xiv., xv.
Aceldama, 9, 18, 80, 86.
Adullam, Cave of, 127, 130.
Ai, 138.
Ain Karim (Convent of St. John Baptist), 112.
Ajalon, Vale of, xx.
Akra, 63, 64.
Aksa, Mosque el-, 17, 25, 32, 55.
Alhambra, 52.
Alkazar, 52.
Aly, Wady, xx.
Amwas (Emmaus?), xx.
Angel, Chapel of, 76.
Anne, St., Church of, 22, 47, 67.
Antonia, Fortress of, 44, 60, 67.
Apparition, Place of, 77.
Aqueducts, 133.
Arabs, 128.
Araunah, 51.
Arimathea, 81.
Armenian Convent, 25, 77.
Armenian Convent at Joppa, vi.
Ascension, Church of, 98.
Ascension, Place of, 106.
Asmonæan Princes, 36, 64.
Assyria, 80.
Athens, 22, 61, 67.

BAALBEK, 22, 60.
Babylon, 79, 80.
Barclay, Miss, 84.
Bead-sellers, vi., 121.
Beautiful Gate, 60.
Beeroth, 145.
Beit Hanina, xxi., 139.
Bethany, 59, 97, 107.
Bethel, 146.
Bethesda, Pool of, 67, 97.
Beth-horon, 144.
Bethlehem, 113.
Bozrah, 67.

Bridge of Temple, 34, 39.

CÆSAREA, v.
Calvary, 67, 75.
Carmel, v., xv.
Chaldea, 80.
Church of Sepulchre, 15, 18, 59, 71, 77.
Cloisters, Royal, 30.
Cœnaculum, 83.
Constantine, 28, 75.
Corinthian Columns, 28, 55, 65.
Court, Inner, 56.
Court of Gentiles, 56.
Court of the Priests, 56.
Crucifixion, 77, 78.
Crusades, 68, 79.

DAMASCUS, 56, 60, 62, 67, 71.
Damascus Gate, 63, 64.
David, 9, 22, 43, 48, 55, 62, 71, 79, 104.
David, Castle of, 25.
David, City of, 14, 62, 63, 81.
David in Wilderness, 130.
David, Palace of, 13.
David, Tomb of, 80, 83.
David, Tower of, 13, 18, 79.
Dead Sea, 13.
Diospolis (Lydda), xvii., xix.
Dives, House of, 67.
Dome of Chain, 55.
Dome of Elias, 55.
Dome of Solomon, 55.
Dome of the Rock, 22, 56.

EGYPT, 81.
Egyptian Colonists, x.
Egyptian Music Girl, xiii.
Elias, 48, 114.
Elisha, 81.
Elizabeth, House of, 112.
El-Mahdi, 55.
Emmaus, xx., xxi. (See Kirjath-jearim.)
En-Gedi, 62.
En-Rogel, 21, 61, 81.
Ephratah (Bethlehem), 113.
Etam, 131.

FOUNTAIN OF THE VIRGIN, 93.

GABRIEL, 48, 51.
Gaza, v.
Geba, 155.
Gebal, 27.
Gebalites, 27.
Gehenna (Hinnom Valley), 86.
George, St., Church of, xviii., xix.
Gethsemane, 9, 10, 101, 103.
Gezer, xx.
Gibeah of Saul, 162.
Gibeon, 138.
Gibeonites, xx.
Gihon, Pools of, 63, 113.
Godfrey, 80.
Golden Gate, 28.
Golgotha, 72, 77.
Grotto of Jeremiah, 67.

HÂKIM, KHALIF, 75.
Haram Area, 17, 22, 25, 28, 29, 31, 32, 33, 35, 36, 39, 44, 61, 64, 67, 68.
Hebron, 80.
Hebron, Gate of, 63.
Helena, Tomb of, 92.
Herod, 30, 31, 36, 39, 61, 68, 79, 80.
Herod, City of, 79.
Herod, Temple of, 60, 61.
Hezekiah, 9, 63.
Hezekiah, Pool of, 14.
Hinnom, Valley of, 9, 13, 61, 63, 78, 81, 85.
Hippicus, Tower of, 79.
Hiram, v., 27.
Holy City, 78, 80, 83.
Holy of Holies, 61.
House Top, Prayer on, v.
Huldah Gates, 32.
Hunt, Holman, Pictures of, 21, 86.

INVENTION OF THE CROSS, CHAPEL OF, 77.
Isaiah, Tree of, 29, 63, 82.

JAFFA GATE, 63.
James, St., Tomb of, 89.
Japho (Joppa), ix.

INDEX.

Jebus, 62.
Jebusites, 13, 22, 62.
Jehoshaphat, Valley of, 13, 29.
Jeremiah, 25, 82.
Jerome, St., Grotto of, 61, 122.
Jerusalem, i., xxii., 9.
Jerusalem, City of, 67, 68.
Jerusalem from the North, 17.
Jerusalem, Site of, 13.
Jerusalem, View of, from Olivet, 18.
Jerusalem, Walls of, 26.
Jewish Tombs, 80, 89.
John, St., 82.
John, St., Baptist, Convent of, 112.
Jonah, ix.
Jonathan, Adventure of, 155.
Joppa to Jerusalem, i., x.
Jordan, 13.
Josephus, 30, 32, 36, 39.
Judges, Tombs of, 92, 139.
Judgment Hall, Pilate's, 67.
Judgment, Valley of, 28.
Justinian, Church of, 55.

KIDRON, 9, 10, 13, 17, 18, 22, 29, 30, 31, 51, 61, 67, 78, 81.
King's Garden, 94.
Kings, Tombs of, 91, 92.
Kirjath-jearim (Kuryet el-Enab), xx., xxi.
Kubbet es-Sukhrah, or "Dome of the Rock," 48.

LATRÔN, xx.
Lazarus, Tomb of, 81, 82.
Lebanon, 27.
Lydda, xvii.

MACHPELAH, 80.
Mediterranean, i.
Melchizedek, 9, 13, 31, 43, 62.
Michmash, Battle of, 156.
Mizpeh, 18, 138.
Moab, 14.
Mocking, Chapel of, 77.
Moors, Gate of, 34.
Moriah, 9, 13, 14, 17, 22, 25, 31, 34, 39, 43, 48, 51, 61, 78, 81.
Mosque el-Aksa, 55.
Mosque, Great, 9, 18, 22, 34, 52, 55, 61.
Musahny, Tomb of El, 92.
Music in Palestine, xiii.
Muslem Cemetery, 28.
Muslems, 14, 15, 22, 25.

NAAMAN, 63.
Nativity, Church of, 59, 124.
Neby Samwil (Mizpeh), 139.
Nehemiah, 32, 44.
Nethinim, Dwellings of, 32.

Noble Sanctuary, 22.
Nob, Site of, 163.

OLIVET, 9, 14, 17, 18, 21, 22, 25, 29, 30, 60, 78, 81, 97.
Olivet, View from, 18.
Omar, Mosque and Traditions of, 13, 14, 15, 48, 56, 61.
Ophel, 32, 34, 55, 94.
Orange Groves, x.
Ornan, Threshing-floor of, 22.

PALACE OF PILATE, 39.
Palace on Zion, 60.
Palestine, 81, 82.
Palmyra, 22, 60, 67, 81.
Peter, St., xv., xviii., 81.
Philistia, xv.
Philistines, ii., xv., 156.
Phœnician Letters on Stones of Temple, 27, 29, 31.
Phœnicians, v.
Pilate, House of, 67.
Pilate's Judgment Hall, 44.
Pinnacle of Temple, 29, 30, 31, 60.
Place of Wailing, 39.
Plague Gallery, Joppa, vi.
Pool of Siloam, 94.
Pool of Sultan, 63.
Pools of Solomon, 132.
Porch of Solomon, 30, 60.
Prophecy fulfilled, 10, 25, 40, 52, 104.
Prophets, Tombs of, 90.

RACHEL, TOMB OF, 115.
Ramah, xvi., 80.
Ramleh, xv., xvi.
Richard, King, x., 141.
Rimmon, Temple of, 60.
Robinson's Arch, 39.
Royal Palace, 34, 39, 78.
Royal Porch, 60.
Ruth, 14.

SACRED ROCK, 56.
Saladin, 56.
Salem, 9, 62.
Samson, 131.
Saracenic Architecture, 47.
Saracenic Wall, 31.
Saracenic Workmanship, 55.
Saul, 71.
Scopus, 17, 81.
Seddon's Pictures of Kidron Valley, 18, 86.
Sepulchre, Church of, 15, 18, 59, 71, 72, 77, 78.
Sepulchre, Holy, 76, 77, 81.
Sharon, Plain of, ii., xv.
Shebna, 34, 82.

Shepherds' Fields, 119.
Siloam, 9, 18, 21, 22, 87, 93, 94.
Simon, House of, v.
Site of the Temple, 51.
Solomon, 22, 48, 79.
Solomon, City of, 79.
Solomon's Ascent to the Temple, 39.
Solomon's Pools, 63, 132.
Solomon, Stables of, 31, 68.
Solomon, Temple of, 27, 39.
St. Stephen's Gate, 61, 67.
Sun, Temple of, 22, 60.
Synagogue, 18.

TAAMIRAH ARABS, 128, 129.
Taamirah Women, 134.
Templars, 55.
Temple, 9, 10, 21, 22, 31, 35, 36, 39, 62, 78, 104.
Temple and Courts, 43, 79.
Temple Court, 34, 39, 60.
Temple Mount, 61.
Temple of Herod, 39.
Temple, Second, 39.
Temptation, Scene of, 120.
Titus, 17, 39.
Tomb of Kings, 17, 91.
Tombs of Jerusalem, 78.
Tombs of Prophets, 90.
Tophet, 9, 13, 80, 85.
Triumphal Entry of our Lord, 108.
Tyre, 27, 67.
Tyropœon, 14, 25, 31, 34, 52, 60, 61.

UNCTION, STONE OF, 79.
Upper City, 62.
Upper Market, 62.
Urtas (Etam), 131.

VIA DOLOROSA, 47, 67, 75.
Virgin, Church of, 25.
Virgin, Fountain of, 93.
Virgin, Tomb of, 90.

WADY ALY, xx.
Well of the Leaf, 56.
Wilderness of Judah, 120.
Women of East, Costume of, ix., 124.
Women of East, Ornaments of, xiv.

YALO (AJALON), xx.

ZACHARIAS, HOUSE OF, 112.
Zacharias, Tomb of, 89.
Zedekiah, 82.
Zion, 9, 14, 21, 22, 25, 29, 34, 35, 36, 39, 52, 61, 62, 68, 72, 79, 81.
Zion, Castle of, 62.
Zion Gate, 62, 63.

December 1886.

IMPORTANT ANNOUNCEMENT.

Completion of the Library and Presentation Edition of

The Land and The Book.

Biblical Illustrations Drawn from the Manners and Customs, the Scenes and Scenery, of

THE HOLY LAND.

By *WILLIAM M. THOMSON, D.D.,*

Forty-five Years a Missionary in Syria and Palestine.

The Volumes are entitled—

I. Southern Palestine and Jerusalem.

With 140 Illustrations and Maps. Imperial 8vo. 592 pages. Cloth extra, richly gilt side, back, and edges. 21s.

II. Central Palestine and Phoenicia.

With 130 Illustrations and Maps. Imperial 8vo. 714 pages. Cloth extra, richly gilt side, back, and edges. 21s.

III. Lebanon, Damascus, and Beyond Jordan.

With 147 Illustrations and Maps. Imperial 8vo. 745 pages. Cloth extra, richly gilt side, back, and edges. 21s.

∗∗∗ Dr. THOMSON has traversed and retraversed the scenes which he describes so graphically, and in these Volumes we have the ripe result of nearly fifty years of careful observation.

The Complete Work is comprised in Three Volumes, Price Three Guineas.

Extract from Preface.

DURING the last thirty years the attention of the Christian world has been directed to the Holy Land in ways and to an extent heretofore unknown. Learned and scientific explorers have penetrated every part of it, and given to the public the results of their researches. Commentaries, Bible dictionaries, books of travel, maps, plans, guide-books, pictures, and photographs have been greatly multiplied. The Palestine Exploration Fund of England has made a thorough survey of Palestine proper, and the American Exploration Society has sent several expeditions to the regions east of the Jordan and the Dead Sea. In these and in other ways a great amount of new information in regard to Bible Lands and the Bible itself has been accumulated; and the author has endeavoured to incorporate in this work the most valuable results of modern research and discovery.

The Land and the Book constitute the all-perfect text of the Word of God, and can be best studied together. To read the one by the light of the other has been the privilege of the author for more than forty years, and the governing purpose in publishing is to furnish additional facilities for this delightful study to those who have not been thus favoured.

The sites and scenes described in the work were visited many times during the author's long residence in the country; and the results, so far as they bear on Biblical illustrations, appear in the current narrative. The conversations are held in the open country, on horseback, by the way-side, or beneath the travellers' tent, and the reader is at liberty to regard himself as the *compagnon de voyage*; for, in the mind of the author, his fellow-traveller is not a mythical abstraction, whose office is merely to introduce new themes, but a real and true-hearted friend, in full sympathy with the purpose and aim of our pilgrimage through the Holy Land.

Any work designed to meet the wants of those who now daily search the Scriptures should abound in illustrations, both textual and pictorial, which are accurate and reliable in detail, and the information imparted must be brought down to the present day. No effort has been spared which was found necessary to reach such a result. The pictorial illustrations are entirely new, prepared specially for this work from photographs taken by the author, and from the best existing materials, and they have been drawn and engraved, under his superintendence, by artists in London, Paris, and New York.

W. M. T.

Mr. SPURGEON says,—"'The Land and the Book' is, to our mind, the best of all books upon the Holy Land; and the Messrs. Nelson have now produced the best edition of it."

Some Opinions of the Press.

British Quarterly Review.—"Its great charm is the picturesque eye and the personal sympathies which, combined with the adequate learning, patient research, and exceptional opportunities of the author, make the book read like a romance."

The Record.—"Incorporates the most valuable results of modern research and discovery with the keen, accurate, and pictorial observations of one who has spent a lifetime in the country itself."

Literary Churchman.—"Among the great number of books upon Eastern 'manners and customs, scenes and scenery,' none probably has assimilated more of the *genius loci*, or is better worth attentive study, than this one. This handsome Work is due to the pen of a gentleman who has himself lived for more than forty years in the lands which he describes."

Nonconformist.—"Dr. Thomson is effective, and clear, and simple, without affecting the picturesque, and gathers up general impressions, and presents them in a vivid and graceful manner...... The illustrations are for the most part simply exquisite......Altogether, it is one of the most beautiful and valuable illustrated books we have yet seen."

Sunday School Chronicle.—"Not content with the experience gained from his long residence and observation amidst the scenes and scenery described, he has incorporated all that has been brought to light by the Palestine Exploration Fund and the researches of the most recent travellers."

Morning Post.—"Can be warmly recommended to the Biblical student......The Biblical and historical comments are ample and good, and the excellent wood engravings tend greatly to enhance the interest of the work."

Daily Review.—"This will now be emphatically *the book* on the subject for popular use......Its value is greatly enhanced by its splendid illustrations."

The Scotsman.—"Full of valuable and trustworthy information, and written with great clearness and ability. The author has sought to strengthen his descriptions of scenery and places by apt Scriptural quotations, and he has produced a book full of a spirit of undoubtedly earnest piety...... The illustrations are numerous and excellent......It has been got up with all the care that has marked the press of Messrs. Nelson and Sons; and, altogether, it is a book of more than ordinary value, and upon which it is certain more than ordinary value will be set by those who may be fortunate enough to obtain it."

North British Daily Mail.—"No writer has brought to his task the unequalled knowledge of the ever-fascinating subject possessed by Dr. Thomson, who was for forty-five years a missionary in Syria and Palestine. His book will always occupy the foremost place among works of this class in the Christian household. No effort has been spared by the publishers to render it as attractive in respect of illustrations as its intrinsic value deserves."

Aberdeen Free Press.—"A work of very great interest and value. Its great charm is the evidence it affords of the author's exceptionally intimate knowledge of life and manners in the East."

Dundee Advertiser.—"Not one of all the many hand-books to Palestine is, in our opinion, equal to this. The author's style is so easy, familiar, and clear, that his vast store of information becomes the possession of his reader before he is aware of the fact. No present more valuable could be given by a Bible class to a teacher than this standard work."

Dundee Courier.—"Dr. Thomson is well qualified to write with intelligence and authority respecting Palestine......Any intelligent person reading and studying the Bible with the help to be derived from such a work as this does so under the most advantageous circumstances, and with a flood of light shed upon many passages which would otherwise be obscure and difficult to interpret."

Thomas Nelson and Sons, London, Edinburgh, and New York.

Southern Palestine and Jerusalem.

SYNOPSIS OF CONTENTS.

I. JERUSALEM TO BETHLEHEM.
II. BETHLEHEM TO EL BIREH.
III. EL BIREH TO NABLUS.
IV. SAMARIA AND THE SAMARITANS—SHECHEM.
V. NABLUS TO ZER'IN.
VI. ZER'IN TO HAIFA.
VII. HAIFA TO ACRE.
VIII. ACRE TO NAZARETH.
IX. FROM NAZARETH TO TIBERIAS.
X. TIBERIAS.
XI. TIBERIAS TO 'AIN ET TINY.
XII. 'AIN ET TINY TO BANIAS.
XIII. BANIAS TO KHAN HASBEIYA.
XIV. KHAN HASBEIYA TO SAFED.
XV. SAFED TO TYRE.
XVI. TYRE AND SIDON.

Central Palestine and Phoenicia.

SYNOPSIS OF CONTENTS.

I. JAFFA.
II. JAFFA TO CÆSAREA.
III. CÆSAREA TO RAMLEH.
IV. RAMLEH.
V. RAMLEH TO ASHDOD.
VI. ASHDOD TO GAZA.
VII. GAZA TO BEIT JIBRIN.
VIII. BEIT JIBRIN.
IX. BEIT JIBRIN TO HEBRON.
X. HEBRON.
XI. HEBRON TO SANTA SABA.
XII. SANTA SABA TO JERICHO.
XIII. JERICHO TO JERUSALEM.
XIV. THE MOUNT OF OLIVES.
XV. THE MOUNT OF OLIVES.
XVI. THE MOUNT OF OLIVES.
XVII. THE MOUNT OF OLIVES.

Lebanon, Damascus, and Beyond Jordan.

SYNOPSIS OF CONTENTS.

I. SIDON TO BEIRUT.
II. BEIRUT.
III. THE DOG RIVER, AND THE SUBURBS OF BEIRUT.
IV. BEIRUT TO SHEMLAN.
V. TOUR THROUGH SOUTHERN LEBANON.
VI. SHEMLAN TO THE NATURAL BRIDGE.
VII. THE NATURAL BRIDGE TO THE CEDARS.
VIII. THE CEDARS TO HURMUL AND BA'ALBEK.
IX. BA'ALBEK TO DAMASCUS.
X. DAMASCUS.
XI. DAMASCUS TO EL MUSMEIH.
XII. EL MUSMEIH TO EDHRA' AND KUNAWAT.
XIII. KUNAWAT TO EL BUSRAH.
XIV. EL BUSRAH TO DER'A AND JERASH.
XV. JERASH TO 'AJLUN, AND ES SALT.
XVI. ES SALT TO 'AMMAN.
XVII. 'AMMAN TO 'AYUN MUSA.
XVIII. THE FOUNTAINS OF MOSES TO THE FORD OF THE JORDAN NEAR JERICHO.

Published by Thomas Nelson and Sons, London, Edinburgh, and New York.

Recent Opinions of the Press.

The Times.—"The large illustrated edition of 'The Land and the Book' has now been completed by the publication of the third volume. We have long been familiar with former editions of the work, and have found it as picturesquely fascinating as it is exhaustively comprehensive. Ordinary travellers in the Holy Land can only give the results of their cursory impressions and observations. Dr. Thomson passed forty-five years in the country as a resident missionary. He rode over it in its length and breadth, he lived with the people, he learned to speak their languages, and he was indefatigable in his efforts at identifying the sacred sites. As he tells us, a great part of the pages were written in the open country—'on seashore or sacred lake, on hill-side or mountain-top, under the olive or the oak, or the shadow of a great rock.' And that we might have imagined, from the freshness of the style and the wonderful vividness of the spirited descriptions. His first volume treats of Southern Palestine and Jerusalem; his second, of Central Palestine and Phœnicia, with which he is specially well acquainted; the third, and the concluding volume, takes a wider and more adventurous range, carrying us round by Damascus, over the heights of the Lebanon, and among the great ruins of Gilead, and the wild nomads in the lawless lands beyond the Jordan. He has incorporated the results of the recent researches and discoveries by the Palestine Exploration Fund and the American Exploration Society. All three volumes are profusely illustrated from photographs taken by himself, which have been drawn and engraved under his superintendence in London, Paris, and New York, and it would be difficult to select a more delightful gift-book."—*Dec. 26, 1885.*

Daily News.—"The completion of Dr. W. M. Thomson's extensive work, entitled 'The Land and the Book,' by the publication of another handsome imperial octavo corresponding with its two predecessors, is an event upon which all who are interested in the topography, Biblical associations, history, life, and manners of the people of the Holy Land may fairly be congratulated. 'Lebanon, Damascus, and Beyond Jordan' is the special title of this section. Few living writers probably have enjoyed the means of studying this vast subject on the spot to the same extent as Dr. Thomson, whose forty-five years of labours as a missionary in Syria and Palestine have furnished the foundation of this work, the archæological researches of the American and English Palestine Exploration Societies providing further and valuable materials. The numerous interesting pictorial illustrations of manners and customs have, we learn, all been designed from photographs of living subjects. Dr. Thomson's lucid and unaffected style of narrative and description, and his painstaking efforts to bring the work up to the level of those studies and explorations which have practically rendered even comparatively recent writers obsolete, are not likely to miss due recognition. A word of acknowledgment must be added for the copious and valuable index of names as well as of subjects and texts. Like its predecessors, the volume is handsomely bound in ornamental cloth, and printed upon fine thick paper with gilt edges."—*Dec. 22, 1885.*

Scotsman.—"The third and last volume of Dr. Thomson's ample and instructive work, 'The Land and the Book,' will be a welcome addition to the library of the Biblical student and of all readers who take an interest in Eastern scenery, peoples, and manners. The previous volumes described 'Southern Palestine and Jerusalem' and 'Central Palestine and Phœnicia.' Dr. Thomson closes his labour with a description of 'Lebanon, Damascus, and Beyond Jordan.' Starting from Sidon, he proceeds along the coast to Beirut. The latter place and its suburbs are described at length in the second and third chapters. Then he turns inland, visiting Shemlan and the Southern Lebanon, viewing 'the cedars,' and passing across Cœlesyria to Ba'albek. From Ba'albek we are taken to Damascus and the region beyond Jordan, and end the tour by viewing Palestine, or discovering how little of it we can view, along with Moses from Mount Pisgah. It is superfluous to say that the volume is full of interest from the first page to the last. Dr. Thomson describes what he has seen, and seen, as a rule, oftener than once. He writes of places and customs with which long residence, much travel, and keen and studious attention have made him familiar; and of peoples whom he has known. His observations, like his book, have had for their great object to perfect acquaintance with and understanding of the Bible in so far as it takes colour from the land of its origin. But his ruling idea is kept in due subjection to reason and fact, and does not lead him to adopt hasty identifications or dubious traditions without critical doubt and inquiry. It is true that the countries here described lie generally outside of the lands of the Bible, taken in a strict sense; but not only do the Bible narratives make occasional excursions into them, but the Scriptures are full of images and allusions which have reference to the peoples and natural features of these countries. The fact that this volume is descriptive of places outside of Palestine accounts for much of the freshness and interest of its pages. The ground covered has not been beaten by so many feet; and though Dr. Thomson's familiarity with the country enables him to charm and instruct his readers even when writing of things and places that have often been visited and described, yet the portions of his work which deal with more rarely visited tracts gain a certain advantage from the reader's comparative ignorance……Of the descriptions of natural scenery, among the most interesting is that of the grottoes of Nahr el Kelb—the caves of Lebanon. The caves have been visited and partly explored by other travellers, but Dr. Thomson's description and the engravings with which it is accompanied will convey to the reader a striking picture of those remarkable grottoes, which are as far beyond comparison with the Derbyshire caverns as they themselves fall short of the caves of Kentucky. The Lebanon country and the 'cedars' are vividly described, and there is a most instructive account of that strange heretical race of Moslems, the Druses. The manners, customs, and peculiarities of the people are treated of as fully as is the natural scenery, and the many excellent engravings serve at once to adorn the volume and assist the reader's imagination. A careful study of this volume will, it might almost be said, convey a more useful idea of much that characterizes the lands it describes than such a rapid tour as most travellers confine themselves to……The book is accompanied with two carefully prepared indexes, in one of which are cited all the Scriptural passages illustrated in the body of the work. The other is an index of subjects; and both, together make this a most valuable book of reference for the Biblical student. It must be added that it is got up in the best style which characterizes the firm of Messrs. Nelson and Sons, and is an exceedingly handsome volume." —*Dec. 12, 1885.*

The Spectator.—"We have received the third volume of the handsome illustrated edition of 'The Land and the Book,' by W. M. Thomson, D.D. This third volume is devoted to what may be called the outlying parts of the Holy Land, 'Lebanon, Damascus, and Beyond Jordan.' Damascus, indeed, was never a part of it, and the same may be said of other localities which Dr. Thomson describes. But they were closely connected with its history, from Abraham downwards. Dr. Thomson starts in this volume from Sidon, and finishes his journey at Jericho. It is needless to say anything in praise of a work to which the author's thorough acquaintance with his subject and indefatigable industry have given a standard value; but we may say that the copious illustrations with which this edition is furnished make it specially desirable."—*Jan. 23, 1886.*

Glasgow Herald.—"Although Dr. Thomson's work is very lengthy it is always pleasant reading—never dry or dull. It forms a most valuable commentary upon Scripture, and enables us to realize clearly and distinctly the meaning of many phrases and references in the Bible which would otherwise be dark and difficult to understand. It is only necessary to add that the externals of this volume are very handsome, and that the printer's work is excellently done."—*Jan. 5, 1886.*

Thomas Nelson and Sons, London, Edinburgh, and New York.

www.ingramcontent.com/pod-product-compliance
Lightning Source LLC
Chambersburg PA
CBHW080503110426
42742CB00017B/2981